PLAZA

Bloom's

GUIDES

George Orwell's
1984

1984
All the Pretty Horses
Beloved
Brave New World
Cry, the Beloved Country
Death of a Salesman
Hamlet
The Handmaid's Tale
The House on Mango Street
I Know Why the Caged Bird Sings
The Scarlet Letter
To Kill a Mockingbird

Bloom's

GUIDES

George Orwell's
1984

Edited & with an Introduction
by Harold Bloom

CHELSEA HOUSE
PUBLISHERS
An imprint of Infobase Publishing

Bloom's Guides: 1984

Chelsea House
An imprint of Infobase Publishing
132 West 31st Street
New York NY 10001

Library of Congress Cataloging-in-Publication Data

George Orwell's 1984 / edited and with an introduction by Harold Bloom.
   p. cm. — (Bloom's guides)
  Summary: Examines different aspects of Orwell's anti-utopian classic, with a biographical sketch of the author and critical essays on this work.
  Includes bibliographical references and index.
  ISBN 0-7910-7567-2
  1. Orwell, George, 1903-1950. Nineteen eighty-four. 2. Science fiction, English—History and criticism. 3. Dystopias in literature. [1. Orwell, George, 1903-1950. Nineteen eighty-four. 2. Science fiction—History and criticism.] I. Bloom, Harold. II. Series. PR6029.R8 N494 2003 823'.912—dc22
                    2003019984

Contributing editor: Gabriel Welsch
Cover design by Takeshi Takahashi

Printed in the United States of America

Bang EJB 10 9 8 7 6 5 4 3 2

This book is printed on acid-free paper.

Contents

Introduction

Rereading *Nineteen Eighty-Four* presents problems not altogether present from 1949, the book's date of publication, on through some thirty-five years later, its projected date of fulfillment. Orwell died in 1950 of tuberculosis when he was only forty-six. Whether in coming years we will judge *Nineteen Eighty-Four* to have been an accurate prophecy is still uncertain. We have gone further in the technological developments that would make the novel's tyranny even more feasible. Politicians on television nightly instruct us in newspeak and doublethink, and the United Nations, in Liberia and elsewhere, practices "peacekeeping" and creates "safe areas," whose burden might as well be "War is Peace." Hollywood's spate of "dumb" films, of the *Forrest Gump* variety, do proclaim that "Ignorance is Strength," and many of our African-American intellectuals rightly judge Gingrich to be telling them that "Freedom is Slavery," particularly when he has urged restoring to the poor their freedom to starve. Big Brother presumably is not *yet* watching us, and we may yet give up putting Saddam Hussein on-screen for the Two Minutes Hate. Even if we had a Ministry of Truth, it would now probably be underfunded in our zeal to abolish government, that enemy of the sacred profit motive which forms our authentic spirituality, the basis for the Christian Coalition.

In so gladsome a time, *Nineteen Eighty-Four* is not likely to lose relevance. It is, in fact, at best a good "bad book," inept as narrative, and worse than that as characterization. The book continues to have moral force as a political early warning and truly is what I once called it, the *Uncle Tom's Cabin* of our time. Actually, it is aesthetically inferior to Harriet Beecher Stowe's novel. Stowe knew better how to tell a story, and Uncle Tom is a more interesting martyr than Orwell's failed martyr, the drab Winston Smith. I would rather attend to little Eva than to poor Julia, and the insane sadist O'Brien is considerably less impressive than the wicked Simon Legree. Wyndham Lewis sensibly compared Orwell as a writer to H.G. Wells, but Wells was consistently more inventive and entertaining. All this is not said to beat up on *Nineteen Eighty-Four*, but to point out that we do not go on reading the book because Orwell possessed a large talent for prose fiction. He did not; he was a moral and political essayist who had the instincts of a pamphleteer. A great pamphleteer, like Jonathan Swift, is a master of irony and satire. Here again, Orwell plainly is deficient. His literalness defeats his wit, such as it is, and his only ironic gift is as a good parodist of political slogans.

And yet *Nineteen Eighty-Four* survives and will have life whenever we are threatened with totalitarian utopias, whether political, economic, social, or theocratic. "Political correctness," our now-passing rage of liberal conformity, is very much an Orwellian phenomenon, and our universities, wretched parodies of what they are supposed to be, are veritable monuments of newspeak and doublethink. It is very difficult to say whether our current Left or our dominant Right is a more Orwellian grab bag, and our public life is mostly a parade marching toward his Oceania. Preachers of the Third Wave, who so enthrall Gingrich, propose a technology founded purely upon information. Orwell remains superbly valuable because no one warns us better that such a foundation in fact must and will give us only an orgy of disinformation. As hypertext and virtual reality usurp us in the computer era, Orwell's nightmare will come ever closer. Without being a great writer, or even a good novelist, Orwell nevertheless had the courage and foresight to see and tell us where we were going. We are still going there, and *Nineteen Eighty-Four* holds on as an admonition telling us to turn back.

Biographical Sketch

Eric Arthur Blair, who would later become known as George Orwell, was born on June 25, 1903 in Motihari, Bengal, the son of a minor British official in India. He and his sister were taken back to England by their mother when he was two years old. The family was able to save enough money to send its only son to St. Cyprian's, an expensive private school near Eastbourne in East Sussex. There Orwell won scholarships to Wellington and, in 1917, to Eton, where he spent four years. Although an excellent student at St. Cyprian's, Orwell was unhappy there and showed little interest in his studies at Eton. Instead of going on to a university program like most of his classmates, he became an officer in the Indian Imperial Police in Burma.

But Orwell's five years in Burma were dismal; in his first novel, *Burmese Days* (1934), he paints a highly critical portrait of the British community there. He returned to England in 1927, penniless and without prospects. He lived in London for several years and then in Paris, earning only enough money to feed himself. He chronicled his experiences among the world of day laborers, itinerant hop pickers, and restaurant employees in his first published book, *Down and Out in Paris and London* (1933).

Orwell's early ambition was to write "a neat shelf of realistic novels." He became increasingly involved in political debate, though, and throughout the early 1930s his work was more political than literary. Following two minor novels (*A Clergyman's Daughter* [1935] and *Keep the Aspidistra Flying* [1936]), he was commissioned in 1936 to write a book-length report on the living conditions of coal miners in northern England; this study was published by the Left Book Club as *The Road to Wigan Pier* (1937). In the following year Orwell went to Spain to cover the Spanish Civil War, but again his politics supplanted his literary aspirations: he joined, and became a captain in the military branch of a syndicalist party that was fighting the Falangist insurgents. After many months at the front, he was shot through the neck, sustaining a

9

permanent injury to his vocal cords. He returned from his convalescence just in time to find that his faction had been denounced by its Communist partners and was being systematically purged. With his wife of one year, Eileen O' Shaughnessy, he escaped across the border to France and returned to England. In 1938 he published *Homage to Catalonia*, an account of his Spanish adventure.

In 1939 Orwell published a fourth novel, *Coming Up for Air*, as he continued to write political commentary and reviews. Once World War II broke out he joined the Home Guard and began to work for the Indian Division of the British Broadcasting Corporation (BBC), producing presentations of political and literary commentary for broadcast to India—these pieces were published in 1985 as *The War Broadcasts* and *The War Commentaries*. In 1943, after disputes with his superiors over the censorship of war news, he left that position and became a literary editor for the *Tribune*, a left-wing weekly for which for several years he also wrote a column entitled *As I Please*. During this time he composed a brief satirical fable about Stalinism, which after many rejections was published in 1945 as *Animal Farm* and was very well received. In the same year his wife, Eileen, died suddenly. Her death left Orwell, who was now chronically ill, to raise the infant son they had adopted in 1944.

Increasingly hampered by pneumonia, Orwell spent his final years on the island of Jura in the Outer Hebrides, working on his last novel, *Nineteen Eighty-Four* (1949). This embittered and compelling dystopian fantasy seemed to prophesy the totalitarian future, and it was an immediate worldwide success, but Orwell would not survive to reap its rewards. He entered a London hospital for treatment of his tuberculosis late in 1949, and soon thereafter he married a young editorial assistant, Sonia Brownell, in a bedside ceremony. Three months later he suffered severe hemorrhaging in one lung, and on January 21, 1950, Orwell died.

In his short life George Orwell managed to leave several works that would inspire and define debate across the political spectrum for decades. He is also regarded as one of the finest essayists in modern English literature; his *Collected Essays, Journalism and Letters* appeared in four volumes in 1968.

The Story Behind the Story

By June 1949, when *Nineteen Eighty-Four* was published, Orwell's reputation in letters and philosophy was already established; *Animal Farm* had brought him celebrity just four years earlier. *Nineteen Eighty-Four*, published in both England and America with huge initial print runs, was immediately hailed as an important and vital work.

Many critics have speculated on the sources behind Orwell's dystopian work. He was fascinated with Shakespeare's *Macbeth*, and that play is a well-known influence. He had read two similar books, both of which are often taught in tandem with *Nineteen Eighty-Four*: Yevgeny Ivenovich Zamyatin's *We* (1924) and Aldous Huxley's *Brave New World* (1932). Peter Davison and Daphne Patai find echoes of Katharine Burdekin's *Swastika Night* (1937), and several biographers have also noted the influence of Jack London's *Iron Heel* (1908). But *Nineteen Eighty-Four* was fundamentally a product of its author's political experience. Orwell had worked as a journalist on socialist and fascist topics, and his reviewing work had exposed him to the wealth of political literature in publication at the time. Orwell critics have also pointed to numerous moments in the author's life that can be felt in his writing, such as the terrors of preparatory school and his experience with brutality and power in Burma.

Orwell wrote *Nineteen Eighty-Four* toward the end of his career, at a point in his life when many of his experiences and political complexities had aged with him through a decades-long internal contemplation. He did write dozens of articles on literature, contemporary political movements, and war, but his most enduring writing on these subjects would be the fictions produced at the end of his life. To many critics, these works represent the most complete articulation of his political thinking.

Orwell seems to have endured vicious torment at his preparatory school, St. Cyprian's in East Sussex. He describes his time there in *Such, Such Were the Joys* (1947), a long essay that he wrote in tandem with *Nineteen Eighty-Four*. While the experiences he describes reflect a kind of brutality that was common in schools at the time, the Orwell biographer Michael Shelden explores the possible influence of St. Cyprian's on the novel. "It is not the case, by any means," Shelden writes, "that these relatively mild forms of tyranny are worthy of any close comparison with Big Brother's nightmarish rule, but all of these elements helped to give Orwell a certain feel for the life which he describes in the novel, a life which is ultimately the work of his imagination, but which is based on real experience."

As an undergraduate at Eton, Orwell displayed a predilection for satire; some critics have read this as an indication that his motivations for writing were external. He was an imaginative writer already, but his imagination was not the genesis of much of his work. It was his later experiences that would plant the seeds of his fiction.

After leaving Eton in 1922, Orwell took a post in the Indian Imperial Police in Burma. He held this post for five years and did little writing during that time. Much of the brutality and oppression he experienced firsthand happened in Burma. In particular, the tactics of police restraint and combat that appear in *Nineteen Eighty-Four* were tactics that he learned in police training and employed during his time in Burma.

But Orwell's affection for and knowledge of the "proles" came in the years after Burma. Throughout the late 1920s and mid-1930s, Orwell moved from place to place, often living with "the down and outs" in Paris, London, and smaller cities throughout the English Midlands. He deliberately sought the experience of poverty, acquiring tattered clothes and the affectations of "being" poor even though he could have lived in a more middle-class mode. He wrote articles about the people he met and the circumstances in which he met them, culminating in the 1933 book *Down and Out in Paris and London*. A year later, he published the novel *Burmese Days*, a fictional indictment of the British occupation of India. While the two books are considered important in the development of Orwell's sociological and political thinking, critics disagree on their merit as works considered apart from *Nineteen Eighty-Four*.

Throughout the late 1920s and into the 1930s, Orwell held various jobs, wrote professionally on a variety of subjects, and began to publish poetry. He taught for a time at Frays College in Middlesex, worked in a bookstore, and finally, by 1935, was employed regularly as a radio correspondent and announcer. Between the publication of *A Clergyman's Daughter* (1935), a novel about losing faith, and the beginning of World War II, Orwell went on to publish the novels *Keep the Aspidistra Flying* (1936) and *Coming up for Air* (1939), the latter warning, like *Nineteen Eighty-Four*, of a society headed toward destruction. He also published the nonfiction works *The Road to Wigan Pier* (1937), *Homage to Catalonia* (1938, on his experience in the Spanish Civil War), and *Inside the Whale* (1940). He was developing as a writer, both personally and professionally.

Orwell's books before this point had flirted with issues pertinent to left-wing politics in general and socialism in particular, but it was not until 1937 that he became involved directly. The *Road to Wigan Pier* commission for the Left Book Club in 1937 characterizes the political involvements of this period, involvements that both hampered his literary career and laid the groundwork for *Nineteen Eighty-Four*. Orwell went to Spain after writing *Wigan Pier*, with the goal of writing articles about the Spanish Civil War. The conflict in Spain, between the Communist/Socialist movement and fascist military insurgents, showed Orwell a starker reality than did the conflicts in England, and he himself actively entered the fray, enlisting in the anarchist militia of the *Partido Obrero de Unificación Marxista* (Worker's Party of Marxist Unification, or POUM). After being wounded in the throat during street fighting, he learned during his convalescence that the POUM had been charged with being anti-communist and that members were being imprisoned or shot. At the same time, he saw that in spite of the language of communism and the policy of equality, class distinctions persisted even among the anarchists.

He and his wife, Eileen O'Shaughnessy, were able to leave the political failure in Spain, escaping to France and then returning to England. Later, while reflecting for the writing of *Homage to Catalonia*, Orwell wanted to make it clear that his time in Spain had been confused but ultimately honorable. He wanted to correct the perception of the POUM held by much of the Left in England, while simultaneously revealing the horrors he found in Stalinist Communism. The contradictions of political thought and individual action did not escape him. Orwell, too, was capable of the extremes practiced in totalitarian states—he had practiced them in Burma—but he understood his intellectual and emotional biases to be "on the side of the weak against the strong." His work for the POUM had shown him the contradictions of official appearance, doctored news, class conflict, and the basic human desire for power. Lines can easily be drawn to the thematic structure of *Nineteen Eighty-Four*.

In the following years, through World War II, Orwell endured chronic tuberculosis, which would ebb and surge and ultimately prove fatal. He grew more active with leftist politics, particularly as a writer and journalist. He wrote what he dismissed as potboiler work for newspapers and magazines; wartime life had made publishing more novels too difficult. He wanted to enlist and fight against the Nazis, but he was declared medically unfit; his tuberculosis and the throat injury from the Spanish Civil War relegated him to working in local defense groups. He worked for the British Broadcasting Corporation (BBC) for a time, crafting political broadcasts to India, and while there he experienced censorship and what he felt to be the fundamental dishonesty of government-sponsored war coverage. (101, the number of the room in which lurks the "worst thing in the world" in *Nineteen Eighty-Four*, was also the number of the room in which Orwell met with the BBC's Eastern Service Committee.) By 1943, unable to stand working for the BBC any longer, Orwell secured a position as the literary editor of *Tribune*, a left-wing publication which, though it had its own problems, was more in line than the BBC with Orwell's political conscience. Orwell began writing *Nineteen Eighty-Four* in the year following Eileen's death, largely on the island of Jura in the Scottish Hebrides.

Orwell insisted that *Nineteen Eighty-Four* was not prophecy; rather, he intended to warn society of the potential perversions of bureaucracy and the state, the perversions of power that he had witnessed over the previous decade, in a variety of forms, in England and Spain. Nevertheless, when the book appeared, various political groups read it as justifying their own positions. Many socialists were enraged with Orwell, seeing the book as an unfair critique of socialism and a betrayal of their cause. Orwell insisted until his death in 1950, that the book was a warning against corruption in general, regardless of the political system that engenders it.

List of Characters

Winston Smith is a thirty-nine-year-old Outer Party member who, as the book opens, has already committed the thoughtcrime which will inevitably bring about his downfall. He works in the ironically named Ministry of Truth, rewriting newspaper articles to match the Party's version of history. His physical appearance manifests the Party's oppression: he has a varicose ulcer just above his ankle, and he is pale, hunched, and wispily balding. He is legally married, but he and his wife are estranged, though they refuse to endure the negative attention of a divorce. He barely tolerates the low-quality tobacco and gin to which he is basically addicted. Winston has vague recollections of life before Big Brother's domination, and his thoughts turn frequently to his mother, the so-called Golden Country, the nature of truth under Big Brother, and the fact that his rebellion has made him into a kind of walking dead. He hates the ideology and omnipresence of Big Brother, and he begins his rebellion by keeping a diary, writing in the one corner of his apartment which is out of sight of the telescreen. Soon after his initial rebellion, he begins a terrifyingly unsafe love affair with Julia, another member of the Outer Party; they conduct most of their meetings in a neighborhood in which the proles live, over Mr. Charrington's antique store. Perceiving anti–Big Brother sympathies in O'Brien, he and Julia swear allegiance to the Brotherhood, of which they believe O'Brien is a member. This is Winston's most aggressive and outward act of rebellion. His punishment, torture, and eventual reprogramming result from O'Brien's careful and thorough reading of his identity—a prime example of doublethink, for while O'Brien understands that Winston both exists within and rebels against Big Brother, he also believes that there are none who oppose the party.

Julia works in the Fiction Department within the Ministry of Truth. At twenty-six, she is more than a decade younger than Winston and has no recollection of a time before the Party's domination. She wears a sash which identifies her as a member of the Junior Anti-Sex League but also, Winston frequently notes, accentuates "the shapeliness of her hips." Winston initially hates her, disgusted by her zeal during the Two Minutes Hate and suspicious that she is aware of his thoughtcrime and is watching him for behavior she can report. Early in their affair, however, he learns that Julia may be even more cynical than he; although she is a member of a few committees and is frequently at the community center, she has had numerous sexual affairs and is quite experienced in hiding them. Her rebellion is more cynical than Winston's and less philosophical.

O'Brien is a member of the Inner Party—as it turns out, a loyal one. Prior to the time of the novel's events, Winston experiences a dream in which O'Brien says to him, "We shall meet in the place where there is no darkness." O'Brien's role in the end of the novel—inquisitor, torturer, and intellectual voice of the Party—positions him as Winston's most fully developed human antagonist.

Mr. Charrington at first seems to be only the kindly and elderly proprietor of an antique shop. Noting Winston's interest in trinkets from the years just before the Party's rise to dominance, he cultivates a relationship with him. Winston rents a room above Charrington's shop for his assignations with Julia; he does not realize that Charrington is a disguised member of the Thought Police. Charrington monitors Winston's and Julia's actions and discussions through a telescreen hidden behind an engraving of the Church of St. Martin in the Field.

Parsons is the windbag enthusiast of a neighbor whose *duckspeak* sloganeering annoys Winston to no end. Hardly less annoying to Winston are the man's children, who, as members of the Spies, are already fully inculcated in Party rhetoric and behavior. (In fact, it is Parsons' three-year-old daughter who reports him to the Thought Police for saying "down with Big

Brother" in his sleep.) Even on his way to what he understands to be certain death, Parsons equivocates about the Party, saying he understands how it must persevere for the benefit of all. Winston worries occasionally that Parsons will betray him.

Syme, a philologist working on the tenth edition of the Newspeak dictionary, is probably the foremost practitioner of that language. In fact, he is *too* intelligent regarding the manipulations of Newspeak; once his talents have ensured the best working edition of the language, he is arrested by the Thought Police for knowing too much about doublethink to practice it to the benefit of the Party.

Big Brother is the human face of the Party, as well as its leader. No one has seen Big Brother in person, and the only sense of his physicality comes from the ubiquitous posters which show his face and the words BIG BROTHER IS WATCHING YOU. The face is square-jawed and handsome, with a moustache and eyes that seem to follow the viewer wherever he or she may move. All successes and positive products of the mind—inventions, strategies, wisdom—are attributed to Big Brother. While it is not clear whether Big Brother actually exists or existed within the novel, he is a necessary humanization of the Party, and thus he persists.

Emmanuel Goldstein is the antithesis of Big Brother and the hated source of all things contrary to Party dominance and perpetuation. Regardless of whether Oceania is at war with Eurasia or Eastasia, Goldstein is the heretic at the enemy's philosophical core and the target of all negative energy from citizens of Oceania and members of the Party. Whereas Big Brother is blandly handsome as a stereotype of the Caucasian male, Goldstein is described as effeminate, Jewish, "ethnic," and unattractive. Goldstein's existence, like that of Big Brother, is never demonstrated.

Ampleforth works in a cubicle near Winston's in the Ministry of Truth, and the two men are employed in the same capacity.

Winston speculates that he, Ampleforth, and their coworkers are in fact engaged in a kind of competition, preparing multiple revisions of given articles so that the Party can choose its favorite. Winston also worries that Ampleforth may turn him in to the police; but Ampleforth himself is eventually arrested, and Winston later sees him in the Ministry of Love. Ampleforth believes his crime was leaving the word *God* in a rewrite of a Kipling poem—but, he contends, no other rhyme was possible.

Summary and Analysis

Nineteen Eighty-Four is told in three sections, comprising eight, ten, and six chapters respectively. The narration is from the third person, with an omniscience limited to Winston's perspective. The first section covers the beginning of Winston's personal treason, his background, and his hopes. In the second, Winston becomes romantically involved with Julia and the two develop their dual rebellion and their relationship and finally approach O'Brien. Also in the second section, Winston reads literature of the opposition, which helps him to formulate his ideas concerning the Party and the Brotherhood. The third section is dominated by Winston's inevitable capture, torture, and reprogramming and his betrayal of Julia and his own humanity.

Humanity is an important concept to remember in thinking about *Nineteen Eighty-Four*—particularly because the author's own humanity plays a key role in the work's construction. For instance, the critic Peter Davison argues against the prevailing belief of critics and biographers that Orwell simply inverted the final digits of the year in which he finished the book, 1948. Rather, he posits an arithmetical source for the book's title, arguing that Orwell delighted in number games and was accustomed to a world in which the falsification of dates had advantages—and thus the title was a game of sorts but also named a date by which a dystopia might reasonably have come into being. Orwell himself left no known evidence of the title's origin. Critics have begun to suspect, though, that Orwell's life had a greater influence on his work than did his political philosophy. But it can be difficult in Orwell's case even to separate the two, and after the novel's publication he had to fend off attacks from fellow leftists who felt he had betrayed them with a stinging indictment of socialism. "My recent novel is NOT intended as an attack on Socialism," he wrote in a letter shortly after publication. "... I do not believe that the kind of society I describe necessarily *will* arrive, but I believe ... that something resembling it *could* arrive.... The scene of the book is laid in Britain in order to emphasise ... that totalitarianism, *if not fought against*, could triumph anywhere." (*In Front of Your Nose 1945–1950* 502.)

Interestingly, the main text of *Nineteen Eighty-Four* is supplemented by a kind of paratext that saps the humanity of the reading experience itself: an appendix that explains the origins, development, and goals of Newspeak, the principal language of INGSOC. The immediate goal of Newspeak is to reduce the English language to only a few hundred words with functional and extremely narrow meanings; its larger goal is to eliminate dissent by eliminating the ability to express dissent. Bernard Crick, an Orwell biographer and a political scientist, and Joan Weatherly (*q.v.*) consider the appendix a symbol that the novel does not, in a sense, *end*, but loops back on itself, the eternal story of any member of the novel's (non-)culture. The perfunctory nature of the description constructs language as a machine—a characteristically Orwellian denial of the human element.

Section One: The Life and Times of Winston Smith

Many critics find *Nineteen Eighty-Four* flawed and heavy-handed as a novel. Harold Bloom, in his introduction to this volume, suggests that the enduring and important aspect is the novel's *vision*, its craft being merely a vehicle for Orwell's ideology, and not always a seductive one. That said, Orwell as an author is careful to put his narrative elements into order at the outset of the novel. One experiences the smell of "boiled cabbage and old rag mats," and among the novel's earliest visuals is that of the Big Brother poster, which is "too large for indoor display ... [and] tacked to the wall." Orwell's description of this is succinct: "[T]he poster with the enormous face gazed from the wall. It was one of those pictures which are so contrived that the eyes follow you about when you move. BIG BROTHER IS WATCHING YOU, the caption beneath it ran."

Immediately, Orwell's prose establishes an atmosphere of foreboding and contradiction. We learn that the desultory place described is named Victory Mansions and that electricity is down to conserve resources while Party members prepare for Hate Week. Electricity cannot be had for such luxuries as boiled water and elevators, yet it is available to run the telescreens, and a voice rattles off production figures about pig iron without interruption. The telescreen is explained at this point and is revealed to be constantly in operation. In most cases, the voice can never be muted, and even when turned off the screen can convey images to the Thought Police, who may be watching at any time for those behaviors from Party members which reveal treasonous thoughts. Winston's world is colorless and cheerless, save for occasional moments of artificial, state-sanctioned color or enforced cheer.

Winston is home at midday, the hour of thirteen, for lunch. Orwell describes his place of work, the Ministry of Truth (or Minitruth), as an enormous white pyramid rising from the squalor of London. On its façade are inscribed the three slogans, and central tenets, of the Party: "War is Peace," "Freedom is Slavery," and "Ignorance is Strength." Winston's job there is to rewrite news articles and other print material from the past so that history, as the Party recreates it, always accords with current policy. The irony of the ministry's name is repeated in the names and tasks of the other ministries: The Ministry of Peace oversees the constant effort of war with the enemy—alternately Eastasia and Eurasia, depending on the Party's intentions. The Ministry of Love oversees the enforcement of law and order, as well as the reprogramming of wayward Party members. Finally, the Ministry of Plenty oversees economic affairs, specifically rationing and the destruction of surplus goods. Many critics view the paradoxes of the names and the slogans, and their roots in the doctrines behind Newspeak, as the most enduring symbols of Orwell's Party totalitarianism. The utter control of the Party extends to the language itself, the agreed-upon manifestation of expressible thought, with a power so extensive that it can construct truth from logical and philosophical contradiction.

Winston is home at midday—rather than in the cafeteria eating lunch, as is his habit—because he is about to commit the major transgression that will set in motion the events of the book. He is about to begin a diary, a paramount act of thoughtcrime, the stakes of which he does not yet fully appreciate. Simply to steel himself to open the book and begin writing, he must take a stiff drink of Victory Gin, a substance he compares to nitric acid; he follows this with a Victory Cigarette, which is of similar quality. These designations continue the pattern of nominal contradiction in the novel, and they typify the existence of Outer Party members under the rule of Big Brother. (Any loyal Party member, however, would point out that Big Brother does not rule but represents the will of the people, individuals being free to do anything they choose.) The Party tells individuals of the wonders the government provides and its inherent benevolence, while the cruel circumstances and shoddy products reveal the reality that perception is at odds with propaganda. To be aware of both facts and yet continue an insistent belief in the goodness of the Party and its ideology is to engage in *doublethink*, the Newspeak word for the ability to hold two thoughts that, although contradictory, one can insist are true. (An example would be believing oneself to be perfectly free because one is *forced* to believe it; there are no laws in Oceania but legions of acts that are punishable by death.) Doublethink is necessary to an individual's operation as a useful and productive a member of the Party.

Winston's predicament, then, stems from a failure of doublethink. In Ian Watt's view, this failure casts Winston as "Oceania's last humanist," a man about whom "there is nothing at all remarkable ... except for his unique inner life." "Behind ... Winston's inner sense of values," writes Watt, "is the larger idea that individual feeling is the most essential and desirable reality available." (Watt 103, 108) Indeed, it is Winston's inability to reconcile the contradictions inherent in doublethink, along with his disillusionment with the Party, that leads him to seek self-expression. A convenient anomaly in his apartment's design creates a space for treason, literally: at the side of the telescreen, out of range of its vision, exists an alcove in which Winston can barely crouch to write. Dating his entry "April 4th, 1984," he begins a tirade which he recognizes as straight Party thinking. The immediate source of the tirade came earlier in the day, at the Two Minutes Hate, at which Party members energetically focused vituperation and violence on a projected image of Emmanuel Goldstein and his heretical anti-Party ideas. Winston saw both Julia and O'Brien there, and his recollection introduces these characters to the book.

Julia's importance is revealed only later. Winston's initial reaction is to her zeal; it eclipses that of all the others. Moreover, he recently has noticed her near him more than usual. He suspects she is spying on him, waiting for a lapse in his behavior that will enable her to turn him in to the Thought Police. O'Brien's case is different. He is a member of the Inner Party, a group with greater influence and privilege than the harder-working and more anonymous Outer Party, and Winston suspects that he is not as eager to uphold Party doctrine as he appears to be. While Julia is frothing with anger and the entire group of Party members is focused on the images of Goldstein and his stream of anti-Party rhetoric, Winston and O'Brien exchange a glance that Winston takes to indicate sympathy, even complicity, and from which he derives his first measure of hope.

Thus, in the alcove, once Winston recognizes his entry as the Party's words, rather than his own, he starts again; this time "printing in large neat capitals—DOWN WITH BIG BROTHER...." He repeats the thought several times and fills half a page.

He is interrupted by a knock at the door; it is his neighbor, Mrs. Parsons, whose husband is a dull and earnest Outer Party member who, like Winston, works at the Ministry of Truth. Winston follows her across the hall to unclog a sink, and in the Parsons' apartment he encounters the couple's children, who have already been indoctrinated into Party ideals as members of the Spies, a group roughly analogous to the Hitler Youth. The children underscore, early on, the twin presence of fear and observation that is central to the life of a Party member, and their accusations against Winston—they call him a Goldstein—foreshadow the novel's ending. In fact, it is too overt an omen to escape even a character's notice, and thus

Winston himself acknowledges that he is "already dead." His acts have only one possible conclusion in such a totalitarian society. But he persists. This is not out of a desire to undo the Party— for he thinks this could be done only by the proles, and even then only through a logistical miracle—but rather because he remembers a "Golden Time," a time *before* the war and the Party's ascendancy.

As the Party (re)constructs it, the history of Oceania runs roughly as follows: At some time between the end of World War II and the time of the novel's events, the three superpowers were consolidated. What readers know as the West—the United States, Great Britain, and parts of Western Europe—became Oceania, and England was relegated to use as Airstrip One. Eurasia, roughly analogous to the former Soviet bloc, evolved to encompass Russia, Ukraine, Poland, the Balkan states, and much of central Asia. Japan, Korea, China, India, and northern Africa together became Eastasia. The novel's perpetual war is about control of the disputed zones and frontiers not dominated by one of the three powers, places like southern Africa, the Middle East, South and Central America, and the islands of the Pacific. Winston cares about the border wars only inasmuch as they remind him of a world outside the domination of the superpowers. His hope, or his rebellion, stems from a sense that there are fewer and fewer individuals who remember the Golden Time; he is motivated at least in part by his own desire to keep those memories alive.

At home, while Winston is doing his exercises and daydreaming about his rebellion, the state of the Party, and dreams of his mother from the night before, the telescreen interrupts his reverie—chilling proof of the Party's ability to see a person whenever it wishes. The Party's very capacity to track and interrupt underscores and justifies Winston's feeling of living death. In the section following, Winston goes to work; this is his "greatest pleasure," a perversion of the mid-century socialist idea that a society's future is in the hands of its workers. Winston does love his job rewriting history, but it does not sustain him. Nor does it contribute to the health of his society; it is noxious, rather, in that social growth requires historical progression, or at least a consistent story of the past. He manages a fractured doublethink in his work. He is aware of what he is doing and can remember enough of his own experience to know that he is creating layers of untruths, but he nevertheless takes pride in a particularly good use of Newspeak or a particularly difficult and well-crafted restatement.

In this section he also encounters Syme, Orwell's character representation of Newspeak. A philologist working on the newest edition of the Newspeak dictionary, Syme is the one person who best understands Newspeak, its devices, and its goals. The timing of his introduction into the storyline—just as Winston revels in his job and its fictions and at the outset of his rebellion—is important, for Syme also appears after Winston's imprisonment. Tellingly, all the individuals introduced at the beginning of the text, with their wide variety of Party viewpoints and differing levels of enthusiasm, come to the same end: Room 101.

At this point Winston also describes the mechanical production of songs and other entertainment for the proles. His thoughts stay on the proles for some time, as he recalls old London and the songs and rhymes of his youth. He is shocked, though, to remember an encounter with a prostitute; her advanced age and decrepitude stand in stark contrast to all his romantic notions of the bliss of the ignorant proles. Orwell uses these twin images of mechanical production of sentiment and the horror of actual raw human contact to juxtapose the state's machine of ideals with the realities of the people. The memories of the encounter stretch through Winston's workday, and they lead to two important moments in this first section of the story.

First, Winston remembers the one moment in his life in which he held tangible, empirical proof of the lies of the party. The proof was a photograph of the convicted criminals Jones, Aaronson, and Rutherford at a certain Party event; all three had purportedly been on Eurasian soil, committing their crimes, when the photograph was taken. Winston recalls the crisis and his delay in destroying the half-page article torn from the *Times*. He had actually seen the men physically—ruined, obviously brainwashed and brutalized—at the Chestnut Tree Café, a symbol that Orwell uses to conjure treachery and the Golden Time. (It is at the Chestnut Tree Café that Winston himself, reprogrammed for a useful life in the Party, will end the book.)

This recalled scene informs the end of the story, then, and provides a key to Orwell's conception of the self. The Orwellian self depends on the recollections and corresponding ideas that make up an inner life; in Joseph Adelson's words, Winston "believes that he is unique and thus precious in possessing a store of personal memory which defines him, and which cannot be taken away from him." (Adelson 118) The Party's insistence that something *is*, when one can recall or reason that it is *not*, is crystallized in an assertion Winston considers, that two plus two equals five. He knows that two plus two does *not* equal five, but he can imagine the reasoning by which the Party might argue that it does. The philosophy of freedom that he describes in his journal—"Freedom is the freedom to say that two plus two makes four. From that, all else follows."—is one of empiricism, then, which would logically be, and later is revealed to be, strictly against Party policy. The instability of fact appears again toward the novel's end, playing a key role in Winston's eventual reprogramming.

The second moment of importance that follows Winston's recollection of the prostitute is his discovery of Charrington's shop, which he finds while on an expedition into the proles' section of London. To go there at all is a risk, but again, as Winston is a "dead man," risk for him has begun to lose its meaning. He is also enamored of the proles in the abstract, and this tendency to romanticize is important to his visualizing the future.

Inside Charrington's shop, Winston strikes up a conversation, charmed by the ephemera that remind him of the Golden Time and needy after being rebuffed by a senile man he questions about the Golden Time. Winston is particularly taken with a glass paperweight that houses a piece of pink coral, and he buys the paperweight from Charrington. To Winston, the coral will gain considerable symbolic significance.

Charrington shows Winston his upper room, outfitted perfectly as a replica of a bedroom as it might have looked before the revolution. Winston notes immediately that there is no telescreen, and shortly afterward he recognizes an engraving of an old building, now bombed out of existence, which Charrington tells him is the Church of Saint Martin in the Field. Charrington sings the beginning of an old rhyme: "Oranges and lemons, say the bells of Saint Clement's." All Charrington can remember aside from the first line is the ending: "Here comes a lantern to light you to bed, / Here comes the chopper to chop off your head." Outside the shop, ready to return home, Winston realizes he has been spotted by another Outer Party member—the woman who watched him at the Ministry and who he thinks very much wants to turn him in. Once he is out of her sight he heads home, filled with suicidal yearnings, to write in his diary and await his fate.

Section Two: Winston and Julia: Alliance and Rebellion

In the opening scene of the next section, Winston learns that he has nothing to fear from the girl with the dark hair. When they bump into each other in the corridor at the Ministry of Truth, she is able to slip to him a folded square of paper, on which she has written the words "I love you." Simultaneously stunned, terrified, and exhilarated, Winston works to contain his enthusiasm while maneuvering for another communication with the girl. Over the course of several days, the two maintain distance in order to elude the Thought Police, engaging in limited conversations when possible, largely in the canteen. In a particularly ironic moment, they speak while watching a parade of war prisoners being transported into the city; because they are prisoners themselves, at least in the psychological sense, they must arrange a meeting amid the bustle of the crowd, protected by a buffering layer of proles. Orwell presents this isolation within a mass of humanity as both a goal and a symptom of tyranny. The critic Alex Zwerdling discusses the psychopolitics of tyranny, and in particular the use of isolation, in Ejner Jensen's *The Future of* Nineteen Eighty-Four.

Zwerdling argues that the totalitarianism of the novel isolates the individual in order to supplant the family in emotional bonding structures:

> ... [T]he regime strives to become the heir of the moribund family and systematically appropriates the emotional capital of that institution. Its leader, Big Brother, combines the qualities of disciplinarian father and loyal sibling. Even the invented conspiracy against him is called "the Brotherhood." (Zwerdling 95)

Winston and Julia create a romance, then, in a world in which interpersonal bonding is inimical to the interest of the state. Winston's vacant relationship with his wife and the treachery of Parsons' daughter both testify to the success of Big Brother's efforts. When Winston and Julia finally meet in the country, Julia explains that her zeal for the Party's approved enthusiasms is a guise. It soon becomes clear to Winston that this woman, though fifteen years his junior, is far more experienced than he in skirting the system and interested more in manipulating it cynically than in changing it or revealing its flaws. Julia brings black-market chocolate—*real* chocolate, rather than the Party's "brown, crumbly stuff"; while in her company, Winston violates nearly every Party principle and commits the crimes which in his diary he only contemplates. In fact, he characterizes their sexual relationship itself as a political act in which the normative Western moral tradition revering virginity is inverted; he proclaims to Julia, "The more men you've had, the more I love you. Do you understand that?" Sex, then, even as they delight in it, is to be savored not for love or lust, but rather as one more blow against Big Brother. Thus Orwell reveals another stultifying effect of totalitarianism: it turns the socially unacceptable into an instrument of open rebellion.

Zamyatin's *We*, noted as an influence on Orwell's work, advances a similar idea of sexual behavior as a form of resistance. Gorman Beauchamp compares the ways in which the two authors employ this motif:

... [T]he rebellion of the individual against the State, in *1984* as in *We*, is presented as a sexual one, the struggle for instinctual freedom against the enforced conformity of an omniscient, omnipotent *étatisme*. Orwell's Winston Smith, like [Zamyatin's] D-503, is the last Adam, reenacting the myth of the Fall, following his Eve into disobedience against God.... Even more clearly than in [Zamyatin's] United State, the rulers of Oceania have grasped the threat to utopianism posed by man's sexuality and are moving drastically to destroy or displace it. (Beauchamp 293)

As Julia and Winston's affair gains momentum with more meetings and sexual encounters, Orwell's narrative continues to reveal the morality of totalitarianism. Winston tells Julia about his wife, Katherine, and her unyielding Party affiliation and refusal to divorce. He then tells her of an opportunity he had to kill Katherine once while the two were on a hike together, with no witnesses, simply by pushing her from a cliff. When Julia asks whether he is sorry he did not seize the opportunity, Winston replies, "Yes. On the whole, I'm sorry I didn't." As the conversation continues and Winston relates his fatalism, his conviction that he is already dead, Julia disagrees. She expresses a relish for the tangible things of the world, a materialism which is the cynical opposite of the Party's rhetoric toward ideals:

"So long as human beings stay human, death and life are the same thing."

"Oh rubbish! Which would you sooner sleep with, me or a skeleton? Don't you enjoy being alive? Don't you like feeling: This is me, this is my hand, this is my leg, I'm real, I'm solid, I'm alive! Don't you like *this?*"

She twisted herself round and pressed her bosom against him.

It is after this encounter that Winston decides to rent the room above Charrington's shop for the purposes of carrying out the affair. While there, he and Julia revel further in the tangible and the specific. Julia obtains makeup, perfume, coffee, and other items either denied to members of the Outer Party or seen as against Party ideology. She heightens her femininity with the makeup in such a way as to commit acts of individualization and vanity—both of which she knows to be thoughtcrime.

Some time after a sexual encounter, Winston and Julia awaken; Julia shoos away a rat, at which point Winston confesses his profound fear of rats. What neither of them knows is that the engraving of St. Martin's is in fact a telescreen—so Winston has just revealed to the Thought Police that which terrifies him most. In a bit of foreshadowing, Winston recalls, in his terror, a recurring nightmare of darkness, barriers, a wall shielding malevolence. Julia embraces him as he struggles against an overwhelming dread. Afterward, while Julia prepares chocolate to drink, she and Winston speculate on the age of the coral paperweight; the conversation progresses to the picture on the wall, behind which, Julia says, there may be "bugs."

Many critics cite details such as this double meaning and its results in calling Orwell's symbology heavy-handed. The passage concludes with Winston's connecting his and Julia's affair with the fragile coral embedded in the dome of glass, though, brittle and illusory; and this symbolic treatment of tyranny and materiality must be considered more delicate. The *things* in the room are of another existence; their idiosyncratic characteristics cannot be tolerated by a regime obsessed with controlling the thoughts of its populace. As a result, ephemera and image are forbidden, especially if they are of another time, as they lead thought away from state-sanctioned channels. All thought that does not reinforce the Party's platform compromises it.

"Bugs," malevolence, and darkness, then, become agents representing the will of Big Brother, whereas the specific items of the room are the only representations of time past. That those representations are fragile and aging is important to show how the past cannot be attained but can be infinitely changed.

Just as Winston's job is to make of the past what Big Brother desires, so too does the painting-telescreen appropriate that past for the state's ends. Winston and Julia even try to remember fruit, and the fact that they cannot do this illustrates how complete an eradication of the past Big Brother will eventually effect.

On the following day, Syme disappears, and his name is purged from all documents and lists, some of which Winston knows carried his name just two or three days before. While Winston's physical health is improving due to his affair and his resulting lifted spirits, it does not occur to him that his newfound glow might tip off the ever-watchful members of the Upper Party. The very existence of the *locus amoenus* becomes a powerful balm to him when facing the intensifying presence of Big Brother. Winston notes that Hate Week is intensifying. Atrocities happen throughout the city, and Julia casually mentions that the bombs that kill children are probably the work of the Party. Winston is stunned that she can think this and yet not be disturbed by it, for the notion that the government would commit such crimes against its own population grieves him. He decides that the difference in perception is likely due to age, and his feelings of isolation are compounded when he realizes there may not be many others who think as he does, and certainly none in the succeeding generations.

After this realization, Winston encounters O'Brien in the hallway at Minitruth. Under the guise of a conversation about Newspeak, O'Brien arranges to have Winston meet him at his home. Winston's spirits are buoyed by the encounter: "All his life, it seemed to him, he had been waiting for this to happen." Winston feels as though the rebellion about which he and Julia have until this point spoken idly is becoming real, tangible, and active. At this point, his own reservations regarding the Party are overcome by his sense of *living*—a sense is rendered more tragic, and more typical of doublethink, because Winston also realizes and has articulated his sense of being "already dead." "The end was already contained in the beginning."

The thinking about his pending encounter with O'Brien

segues into his next encounter with Julia, during which time he relates to her how, until the moment he is saying it, he always thought he had killed his mother. In reality, she had been made to disappear by the Party, likely sent to a forced-labor camp, but the recollection and realization leads Winston to regard the proles once again as the single collective instrument of hope. Because the proles are like the people of "two generations ago," they see the importance in gestures, in action, whereas in the current life of the Party, the individual makes no difference at all. In conforming to the Party ideal, one becomes anonymous. If one does not conform, one disappears, all traces of one's life eradicated. As such, the Party never wavers and is able to effect a singularity out of many—a singularity which, because of its utter monochrome persistence, allows no emotion or hope or goals which do not encourage its perpetuation. The proles, however, do not participate in the Party. Winston admires their independence: "The proles are human beings. We are not human."

Winston's realization of the proles' more or less *true humanity* leads Winston to beg of Julia that they make their own commitment the thing that matters. Winston tells her that none of their actions will forestall their death, that the only important thing "is that we shouldn't betray one another, although even that can't make the slightest difference." He means that they must not let the Party make them stop loving each other. Naïvely, both aver that the Party cannot do such a thing, that it cannot, as Julia puts it, "get inside" human emotions.

Afterward, Winston and Julia meet O'Brien at his apartment, a place that, though spartan, is far better outfitted than the apartments of other Outer Party members. O'Brien has real coffee, real sugar, soft lighting, papered walls, and a host of other creature comforts. Most importantly, when he greets Winston and Julia, he turns off his telescreen—which no Outer Party member can do. Winston and Julia are stunned.

O'Brien outlines the tenets of the resistance, known only as the Brotherhood, and the group's loyalty to Emmanuel Goldstein, as well as the fact that there is no actual *group*, just an act of faith in its shadowy and collective existence. He then makes Winston swear to take any steps necessary to uphold the Brotherhood, including asking whether Winston would be willing to throw acid in a child's face if the need arose. Winston affirms without hesitation, to each of O'Brien's questions, swearing to a form of extremism little different from that of the Party itself, save that the object of reverence is Goldstein instead of Big Brother. O'Brien is well prepared for Winston; he knows the complete rhyme that begins with the bells of St. Clement's, he knows to assure Winston that "we are the dead," and he makes specific reference to the meeting in a place without darkness. Winston is so overcome with the realization of his dreams that his suspicions, honed during his years with the Party, are suddenly swept aside, and he believes fervently in O'Brien's words.

In the following week, the focus of the ongoing war in which Oceania was engaged changes, imperceptibly to everyone but Winston. The change occurs in the middle of a speaker's sentence on the sixth day of Hate Week. Simply, Oceania was no longer at war with Eurasia. "Oceania was at war with Eastasia; Oceania had always been at war with Eastasia." At the same time, Winston receives Goldstein's book, *The Theory and Practice of Oligarchical Collectivism*, from a Brotherhood member, in the highly secretive and elaborate manner that O'Brien had promised. He reads the book in the room above Charrington's shop.

The book explains the philosophy and practice governing the Party's behavior, and as Winston reads, readers of *Nineteen Eighty-Four* are privy to the same text, one which describes the tangled logic of doublethink; the reasons for perpetual war and its use of every manufacturing and agricultural surplus available; the manipulation of the proles through rhetoric; the Party's reason for wanting power for power's sake; the bodiless manifestation of the Party as an organ of philosophy; and more. (The passages also describe the Machiavellian bent of perverted socialism and eerily predict the Cold War, the arms race of the 1970s and 1980s, and the border skirmishes at the edges of the world's so-called superpowers.)

Goldstein finally explains that for the Party's power to exist there has to be a sense of being entirely a part of it, and not excluded from it. He uses the term *collectivism* to describe the Party's decision to eliminate private property. If everyone owns everything, then the governmental structure is based on a common good and a common set of goals, and everyone gets what he or she requires from the state. However, the flip side of such thinking is that no one owns anything—so no one holds any real stake in such a society.

Winston finishes the book, naps with Julia, and awakens to the sentimental song he hears every time at Charrington's, sung by a prole woman hanging laundry in an alley. While he and Julia lie in golden light from the waning sun, Winston marvels at the potential power of individuality, how a person's single strength, fed on relationships and the secret knowledge of the way things really *were*, could eventually affect a change—how such reason would *have* to overthrow the Party eventually. He knows it will not happen in his or Julia's lifetime, but as long as such people live and keep the knowledge alive, there will be an end to the Party. As he repeats to her their secret phrase, "we are the dead," she repeats it back, and then a third voice, an "iron voice," repeats it as well.

In the ensuing arrest, the telescreen is revealed, Charrington is unmasked as an agent of the Thought Police, the last lines of the rhyme are told to them ("Here come a candle to light you to bed, here comes the chopper to chop off your head!"), and the delicate coral paperweight is smashed by a Party enforcer. The men beat Julia and haul her from the room, and this is the last Winston will ever see of her.

Section Three: Winston Learns to Love Big Brother
Winston too is taken away, to what he believes is an area of the Ministry of Love; he loses his sense of time and place and has no knowledge of Julia's fate. He is hungry, unable to focus his thoughts, and slightly appalled by other people who come in and out of the room he occupies. He waits for what he feels will be certain rescue by the Brotherhood. Ampleforth soon

joins him, unsure of the particulars of his own crime, though he suspects he is imprisoned because he left the word *God* in a rewritten poem. He shrugs off this superficial reasoning: "There is only one offense, is there not?"

Soon, Ampleforth is taken by guards to Room 101; Parsons appears shortly thereafter. Parsons' daughter turned him in, Winston learns, for denouncing Big Brother in his sleep. Parsons' acceptance of his culpability is repellent to Winston and serves as further evidence of the effect of totalitarianism. Parsons, too, is removed to Room 101. The effect of this section of the novel is not complete, however, until O'Brien arrives to take Winston himself away—assuring Winston that he knew, all along, that this would happen. He reminds Winston of his acceptance of fate forgone, that he was the dead, and that both men knew of their eventual meeting in "the place where there is no darkness," the well-lit rooms of Miniluv.

Room 101 is numbered without importance, implying that breaking someone through fear is so much a part of the bureaucratic duties of the Party that it is relegated to one of a number of functional rooms. It is not Room 1, or Room 100, or any location of prominence. Rather, it exists somewhere in the Ministry of Love, anonymous—and Newspeak will, no doubt, eliminate any words to describe it, lest the language make obvious the reason and need for such a room. Some of Orwell's biographers claim that the number represents any number, a number of no specific significance, a number that would cast torture by the state, the worst fears of the citizens realized, as just another mundane business, on par with the adjusted figures for agricultural yields and the need to ensure immunization from diseases. The anonymity of the room constructs the crushing of spirit and individual thought as just another function of a bureaucracy.

Winston is not taken immediately to Room 101, though. When the guards take him, he is clubbed on the arm, rendering that arm useless and returning him to the weakened state of health he had experienced before meeting Julia and participating in active rebellion. The physical deterioration continues during his time in Miniluv. For an indeterminate time, Winston is tortured, made to confess to crimes against the Party, and generally eroded; then O'Brien arrives and begins to work on the limits of Winston's memory. O'Brien has access to a pain device that, unseen, inflicts the most severe pain Winston has ever known. Winston's first taste of its power comes when, after unbearable pain assails him, O'Brien reminds him that the dial goes to one hundred and the setting he has just felt was forty.

O'Brien is telling Winston he is "mentally deranged," a fact evidenced particularly in the delusion Winston has of the photograph of the three Party members "executed for treason," Jones, Aaronson, and Rutherford. O'Brien shows Winston the photograph and then destroys it, whereupon Winston insists that the photograph still exists "in memory." O'Brien counters that the Party controls all manner of the past because it controls the physical evidence of the past, as well as the memories of individuals. When Winston counters that his memory is not under Party control, O'Brien tells him that it is Winston's lack of discipline, of mental ability, that keeps him from being "sane" in the eyes of the Party. This, O'Brien says, is the reason why Winston is in Miniluv—to learn discipline and humility.

O'Brien asks Winston to count the fingers he is holding up; Winston counts four. O'Brien urges him to understand that there may in fact be five or three *or* four, that he needs to be more wary of his senses, as they are weak and subject to illusion. Winston agrees to say whatever O'Brien wishes him to say, but O'Brien replies that he wants Winston to say only what he *believes*. Winston fights, a dogged empiricist, but O'Brien's pain mechanism eventually causes Winston's vision to blur, and he cannot accurately see a static number of fingers to count. He tells O'Brien this; O'Brien responds, "Better." Afterward, O'Brien tells Winston something the imprisoned man has only begun to realize: the Party is not interested in the overt action of a person. Rather, it is interested in the *thoughts* of that person. "We do not merely destroy our enemies," he says; "we change them."

The Party's motivation to change Winston, torturing him in order to do it even though this will destroy him in the end, is not a general desire to wipe out the individual. Rather, it is a desire to wipe out any sentiment or thought against the Party. By aggressive conversion and change the Party eradicates such thought, makes its dominance perfect—and then it need destroy only what is willingly given up.

O'Brien continues to badger Winston for days with logical fallacies, contradictions of perceived reality, and Party rhetoric. Among other revelations, he tells Winston that Julia converted in "a textbook case" and that she betrayed Winston "almost immediately." He also tells Winston that Goldstein's book describes the Party accurately but misattributes the Party's motivation as a desire for revolution. In fact, O'Brien says, the Party's quest was simply for power itself. O'Brien characterizes Winston as the last defender of humanity and urges him to look in a mirror at what that image has become. Of course, Winston is shocked at his decay, his fragility, his utter insubstantiality next to O'Brien.

Afterward, as Winston's reeducation begins to allow him to return to health, he is programmed to the point of accepting all of the tenets of the Party, with the exception of actually loving Big Brother. To remedy this, O'Brien orders that Winston be taken to Room 101, which he tells Winston holds "the worst thing in the world." For Winston, "the worst thing in the world happens to be rats." Winston is locked into a cage of which one section fits his face and another contains rats. A hinge will enable the rats to reach his face. He is mad with fear. The scene ends with his betrayal of Julia; as the rats approach his face, he shouts, "Do it to Julia! Do it to Julia!" Devastating though this betrayal may be, Zwerdling argues that it can come to pass only because Winston wills it:

> Orwell makes it clear that at a deeper level Winston wills his own degradation because of his wish to submit. He knows he will be caught, has no chance of escape, yet deliberately chooses a path that can only lead him to a place where he will be—in his own words—"utterly

without power of any kind.".... And when O'Brien stands revealed not as a fellow conspirator but as an agent of the regime, he says to Winston in words that ring true, "You knew this.... Don't deceive yourself. You did know it—you have always known it." (Zwerdling 100)

Thus Winston's will is not only crushed but entirely rewritten; beyond this point, whether he yearned for conversion or not will be as unknowable and irrelevant as any other historical scrap. Michael P. Zuckert discusses Winston's defeat as a reflection of Orwell's own fear that "collective solipsism," the individual's inability to define reality for himself, was all too apparent in the climate of his time:

Orwell's fixation with "telling the truth" and standing against the crowd, are the response of a man who personally felt the power of the crowd over his own mind. "Confessions" at purge trials, the brazen rewriting of history, inducing conviction in the minds of men by sufficient repetition and control of what can and cannot be said and validated in public spaces-these broader historical experiences of his time must have convinced Orwell that the power of collective solipsism was great indeed. (Zuckert 57)

In the book's final section, Winston sits in the Chestnut Tree Café, where the three treasonous Party members were photographed. He is revealed to be a regular, showing up to play chess under the eye of Big Brother. He has returned to his former poor health, only now he is fatter, balder, rougher, and redder. He still hates the gin, but he has achieved a fretting peace, jumping at the sound of the telescreen, pushing away "false memories" of his mother, and instead realizing that in his changed state, in his new, higher-paying job, he has been broken and is completely a functionary of the Party. In fact, the Party is so confident in his breaking that he realizes, however intuitively, that it is barely concerned with anything he may do. He remembers seeing Julia one more time, out in public; the landscape around them was dull, dirty, blasted. They touched briefly and were repulsed by one another. She said she had betrayed him, and he told her the same. He wanted nothing more than to get away from her. The memory ends, then, as the telescreen makes noise about war and conquest and Winston, with his new job working on a subcommittee of a subcommittee concerned with the eleventh edition of the Newspeak dictionary, with his fervency in the face of the statistics coming from the telescreen, realizes that he loves Big Brother.

The book concludes with an appendix that describes Newspeak, speaking of the year 1984 in the past tense. Such a reference is fitting *dénouement* to Winston's defeat, for it implies the impassive continuance of the Party and its ability to survive any resistance a Winston Smith might offer. It is also told in bland, pseudo-anthropological "Establishmentese," a register of language that renders the actual end of the novel something official, forgettable, plain. Thus the Party's rule is perpetuated, readers are returned to the official version, and the last words sound as though no one like Winston had ever existed.

Works Cited

Adelson, Joseph. "The Self and Memory in *Nineteen Eighty-Four*." *The Future of* Nineteen Eighty-Four, edited by Ejner J. Jensen. Ann Arbor: University of Michigan Press, 1984.

Beauchamp, Gorman. "Of Man's Last Disobedience: Zamyatin's *We* and Orwell's *1984*." *Comparative Literature Studies* 10: 4 (December 1973), pp. 285–301.

Orwell, George. *In Front of Your Nose 1945–1950: The Collected Essays, Journalism and Letters of George Orwell*, edited by Sonia Orwell and Ian Angus. New York: Harcourt Brace and World, Inc., 1968.

Watt, Ian. "Winston Smith: The Last Humanist." *On* Nineteen Eighty-Four, edited by Peter Stansky. New York: W.H. Freeman and Co., 1983.

Weatherly, Joan. "The Death of Big Sister: Orwell's Tragic

Message." *Critical Essays on George Orwell*, edited by Bernard Oldsey and Joseph Browne. Boston: G.K. Hall and Co., 1986.

Zuckert, Michael, P."Orwell's Hopes and Fears." *The Orwellian Moment: Hindsight and Foresight in the Post-1984 World*, edited by Robert L. Savage, James Combs, Dan Nimmo. Fayetteville: University of Arkansas Press, 1989.

Zwerdling, Alex. "Orwell's Psychopolitics." *The Future of Nineteen Eighty-Four*, edited by Ejner J. Jensen. Ann Arbor: University of Michigan Press, 1984.

Critical Views

STEPHEN SPENDER ON MORALITY IN THE NOVEL

[F]or Orwell no return either to tradition or to religion is possible. If society cannot be saved, he is scarcely interested in saving himself from society, and if it is damned, then he pins hope not to his own art or soul but to the unpolitical recklessness of the 'proles'. He was a man more deeply concerned with the political future of society than with his own life or work, though he did not believe, at the end, that any political solution was possible. (...)

In *1984* there has been a purging by Orwell of simplified political good-and-evil.... In the end Big Brother and his Party are not bad because they are politically reactionary or even totalitarian, but because they indulge a lust for power which approaches very nearly to a lust for pure evil. And as in Baudelaire's Paris, the highest possible good in the conditions of *1984* has become a conscious pursuit of sensuality. For where good is impossible, the sins of the senses can be used as a moral weapon against abstract evil. *1984* is a political novel in which politics have been completely purged of current assumptions such as that the Left is good and the Right bad. We are confronted with a world in which any side can use politics as an excuse for plunging the world in evil.

And although there is no Christ in Orwell's world, Big Brother is really anti-Christ. He wills that the whole society shall will nothing except his will, he demands the love of his victims, in their lives and in the manner of their deaths. If the idea of the equality of man is the centre of Orwell's abandoned vision, the idea of the will of Big Brother is the centre of his anti-vision. Thus as we read on we realize that those slogans introduced at the beginning of the book, which at first read like crude parodies, are literally the moral laws of a world where Evil has become the anti-Christ's Good. LOVE IS HATE, WAR IS PEACE, and IGNORANCE IS STRENGTH are the basic principles of belief for the members of the Inner Party, and Winston Smith experiences a feeling of conversion when he is completely convinced that a lie is the truth. He loves Big Brother.

The tragedy of Orwell's world is that man—Big Brother—turns himself into God, but there is no God.

GEORGE ORWELL'S DEFENSE OF HIS NOVEL

[Part of a letter, since lost, written on 16 June 1949 by Orwell to Francis A. Henson of the United Automobile Workers answers questions about *Nineteen Eighty-Four*. Excerpts from the letter were published in *Life*, 25 July 1949, and the *New York Times Book Review*, 31 July 1949; the following is an amalgam of these.]

My recent novel is NOT intended as an attack on Socialism or on the British Labour Party (of which I am a supporter) but as a show-up of the perversions to which a centralised economy is liable and which have already been partly realised in Communism and Fascism. I do not believe that the kind of society I describe necessarily will arrive, but I believe (allowing of course for the fact that the book is a satire) that something resembling it could arrive. I believe also that totalitarian ideas have taken root in the minds of intellectuals everywhere, and I have tried to draw these ideas out to their logical consequences. The scene of the book is laid in Britain in order to emphasise that the English-speaking races are not innately better than anyone else and that totalitarianism, *if not fought against*, could triumph anywhere.

The influence of Zamiatin's work on *1984* is pronounced and pervasive; indeed, one critic has called *We* Orwell's *Holinshed*.[20] Many of the features of the United State reappear in Orwell's Oceania, not least of which is the systematic repression of the sexual drives. Thus the rebellion of the individual against the State, in *1984* as in *We*, is presented as a sexual one, the struggle for instinctual freedom against the enforced conformity of an omniscient, omnipotent *étatisme*. Orwell's Winston Smith, like Zamiatin's D-503, is the last Adam, reenacting the myth of the Fall, following his Eve into disobedience against God.

The topography of Oceania is well enough known that I need not dwell on it: the telescreens, Big Brother's electronic eyes that are always "watching you"; the phenomena of *newspeak* and *doublethink* and *blackwhite*; the ubiquitous slogans proclaiming war to be peace and freedom slavery. Nor need I stress the dystopian nature of Orwell's vision of utopia at dead end, all its perverted values terroristically enforced by the Ministry of Love.[21] What should be pointed out, however, is the remarkably precise way in which Orwell has embodied, in the conditioned hysteria of love for Big Brother, Freud's theory of eroticism displaced. In the daily Two-Minutes Hate (the Oceanic equivalent of prayer), the telescreens project the image of Goldstein, the satan of this State, against whom the increasingly frenzied faithful hurl their hatred. Then (Winston recounts of one such Hate) "drawing a sigh of relief from everybody, the hostile figure melted into the face of Big Brother ... full of power and mysterious calm, and so vast that it filled the screen.... The little sandy-haired woman had flung herself over the chair in front of her. With a tremendous murmur that sounded like 'My savior!' she extended her arms to the screen."[22] Julia, Winston's Eve, explains "the inner meaning of the Party's sexual puritanism."

It was not merely that the sex instinct created a world of its own which was outside the Party's control and which therefore had to be destroyed if possible. What was more important was that sexual privation induced hysteria, which was desirable because it could be transformed into war fever and hero worship. The way she put it was:

"When you make love you're using up energy; and afterwards you feel happy and don't give a damn for anyone. They can't bear you to feel like that. They want you to be bursting with energy all the time. All this marching up and down and cheering and waving flags is simply sex gone sour. If you're happy inside yourself, why should you get excited about Big Brother?" (pp. 110–11)

In order to ensure that the Oceanians do get excited about Big Brother—displace, that is, eroticism from its natural object, another individual, to the State—the Party attempts in every way "to remove all pleasure from the sex act.... The only recognized purpose of marriage was to beget children for the service of the Party. Sexual intercourse was to be looked on as a slightly disgusting operation, like having an enema" (p. 57). Thus the Party instigated organizations like the Junior Anti-Sex League, a sort of celibate Scouts, whose chastity, like that of medieval monks and nuns, demonstrated their superior love for and loyalty to their god. For the Party's ultimate aim, as the Inquisitorial figure O'Brien explains to Winston, is the total abolition of the sex instinct: "We shall abolish the orgasm. Our neurologists are at work upon it now.... There will be no love, except love for Big Brother" (p. 220). Even more clearly than in Zamiatin's United State, the rulers of Oceania have grasped the threat to utopianism posed by man's sexuality and are moving drastically to destroy or displace it.

Notes

20. Christopher Hollis, A *Study of George Orwell* (London, 1956), p. 199. For the most instructive discussions of Orwell's debt to Zamiatin,

and their differences, see Woodcock, "Utopias in Negative[," *The Sewanee Review*, 64:1 (1956)]; Isaac Deutscher, "*1984*—The Mysticism of Cruelty," *Heretics and Renegades* (London, 1955), pp. 35–50; and Jürgen Rühle, *Literature and Revolution*, trans. Jean Steinberg (New York, 1969), pp. 38–40. Orwell himself wrote an appreciative review of *We* in his column in the *Tribune* (London), 4 January 1946.

21. George Kateb in *Utopia and its Enemies* (New York, 1963), pp. 235–36, argues that Oceania ought not to be considered even a negative utopia, for O'Brien "describes the political system of *1984* as ' ...the exact opposite of the hedonistic utopias that old reformers imagined.'" Kateb has a point, but it is rather strained and overly formalistic. Orwell's vision of the future is clearly intended to show utopian messianism gone sour, reflecting the historical reality of our century. Consider the reflection of Koestler's Rubashov: "Nobody foresaw the new mass movements, the great political landslides, nor the twisted roads, the bewildering stages which the Revolutionary State was to go through; at that time one believed that the gates of Utopia stood open, and that mankind stood on its threshold" (p. 106). For an excellent account of the dashing of these bright hopes, see Sir Isaiah Berlin's essay, "Political Ideas in the Twentieth Century," *Four Essays on Liberty* (New York, 1969), pp. 1–40.

22. George Orwell, *1984* (New York, New American Library, n.d.), p. 17.

PAUL R. EHRLICH AND ANNE H. EHRLICH ON POPULATION

The analysis of the environmental aspects of *Nineteen Eighty-Four* that follows is in several respects unfair to George Orwell. Anyone who writes about the future knows that precise prediction is impossible. One can forecast the implications of current trends on the assumption that they will continue; but the forecaster is always aware that many trends are unlikely to continue. We would view *Nineteen Eighty-Four* as a *scenario*, a device used to stimulate thinking about the future implications of the present course of society. In that context it was an enormous success, for, whether it was intended as a forecast or a warning, *Nineteen Eighty-Four* alerted people to certain dehumanizing trends—some of which still seem very threatening today—flowing partly from technological advances.

What struck us most sharply, however, upon rereading *Nineteen Eighty-Four* for its treatment of environmental issues was not Orwell's prescience in this area, but his blindness. In this particular context he was completely a man of his times. But that the same blindness should still afflict many educated people today is frightening. These people have little excuse for their affliction; unlike George Orwell, they live in a society where information on environmental issues is widely available. Environmental blindness allows people to imagine humanity as abstracted from nature and affected only by social phenomena, answerable only to itself and to the gods of its invention. Partly because of this blindness, Orwell's fictional world, created just after World War II, is a poor reflection of the real world of today.

A major theme in *Nineteen Eighty-Four* is the use of perpetual warfare by the Party, not just to generate a continuous war hysteria and thereby manipulate the citizenry more easily, but also to avoid the surpluses that would inevitably be created if peace were to reign. This policy is explicitly stated: "The primary aim of modern warfare ... is to use up the products of the machine without raising the general standard of living.... If the machine were used deliberately for that end, hunger, overwork, illiteracy, and disease could be eliminated within a few generations."

Orwell here appears to have embedded a local partial truth in a global misperception. It is true that one function of military expenditure in either war or peace in real "steel-eating" societies is to accelerate the conversion of natural resources to rubbish—to boost the economy by speeding up throughout. But whether this function could legitimately be called primary, and whether it is ever consciously planned for the purpose of keeping the general standard of living low, are much more problematic.

The operative global misperception is that past triumphs of "the machine" indicate that it has a capacity, in essence, to solve permanently all problems for a human population of indefinite size. This misperception—based in ignorance of physics, chemistry, and biology—is widespread in society even today, as evidenced by the writings of cornucopian economists. Harold Barnett and Chandler Morse, the authors of *Scarcity and Growth*, got the second law of thermodynamics exactly backward and provided the classic statement of the cornucopian position: "Science, by making the resource base more homogeneous, erases the restrictions once thought to reside in the lack of homogeneity. In a neo-Ricardian world, it seems, the particular resources with which one starts increasingly become a matter of indifference." Yet another economist, Mogens Boserup, has chimed in with the opinion that "the entropy story ... is irrelevant ... for human action and policy." At the extreme, the cornucopian position is symbolized by the statement of a professor of advertising, Julian Simon, that the only limit to the amount of copper that could be made available to humanity is "the weight of the universe."

There are, of course, some economists who understand that there are limits on what the machine can accomplish. But this view is as yet accepted by only a minority of the profession and probably of society as a whole. Orwell's mid-century picture of humanity as virtually disconnected from the physical and biological worlds is still all too persistent among the most influential of social scientists.

For much of Orwell's adult life, demographers were concerned that populations in the industrialized world might *decline*. It is not surprising, then, that Orwell paid scant attention to the problems of overpopulation. The demographic history of the thirty-five-year period between 1949, the year *Nineteen Eighty-Four* was published, and the approaching year 1984, has, of course, created conditions totally unlike those Orwell described. He indicated that the nation of Oceania—consisting of Britain, the Americas, Australasia (Australia and New Zealand, presumably), and southern Africa—have a 1984 population of about 300 million. This is actually well under the 1950 population of the Western Hemisphere alone, and far below the roughly 740 million people now living in that "nation."

Orwell's Oceania missed the post–World War II population explosion—arguably the most significant event of the era he was previewing. But there were good reasons why that explosion did not occur in Orwell's world. One was the decrease in reproduction achieved by the repression of sexual activity, as exemplified by the Junior Anti-Sex League; O'Brien states the goals of the Party: "Children will be taken from their mothers at birth, as one takes eggs from a hen. The sex instinct will be eradicated. Procreation will be an annual formality like the renewal of a ration card. We shall abolish the orgasm.... There will be no love, except the love of Big Brother."

Had Orwell been more scientifically oriented, he might have predicted that technological advances would make it possible, as indeed they have, to allow eggs to be taken from women and "hatched" elsewhere. Sex then could have been totally abolished in Oceania. The test-tube baby did not, however, originate in the societies (the Soviet Union and China) that most closely resemble that of *Nineteen Eighty-Four*. The process was first perfected in richer, less repressed nations, not as a step toward state control of reproduction, but as a method of restoring fertility and gaining reproductive freedom.

IAN WATT ON WINSTON SMITH AS THE LAST HUMANIST

At the beginning of *Nineteen Eighty-Four*, we are given a few facts about Winston Smith. He's thirty-nine and has "a varicose ulcer above his right ankle"; on the next page we're told he's a small, frail figure with fair hair, and afraid of the Thought Police; and on the next page we learn that he works for the Ministry of Truth in London, the chief city of Airstrip One, the third most populous province of Oceania. The rest of what we are told about him is fairly consistent with this, and makes it clear that there is nothing at all remarkable about Winston Smith except for his unique inner life.

The first thing we learn about it comes when he tries "to squeeze out some childhood memory that should tell him whether London had always been quite like this." The urgency of the word "squeeze" suggests that Winston Smith's interior consciousness is genuinely tormented by what is essentially a historical question. Winston's first significant act tells us a good deal more. He has left his job at thirteen hours, downed a teacupful of nauseating Victory Gin, and moved to the alcove which, quite exceptionally, is out of sight of the telescreen, having probably been intended originally "to hold bookshelves." Once there he takes out a "peculiarly beautiful book," fits a nib onto an archaic penholder, and begins a diary. Winston Smith's secret life, then, is not merely puzzled by history; it is in love with the products of the past.

Until he started the diary, Winston Smith had imagined that "the actual writing would be easy. All he had to do was to transfer to paper the interminable restless monologue that had been running inside his head, literally for years." But it turns out not to be easy, and the reason for the difficulty is peculiar: "How could you communicate with the future?... Either the future would resemble the present in which case it would not listen to him, or it would be different from it, and his predicament would be meaningless." This surely shows that Winston's consciousness in general is dominated by two different kinds of persistent concern: the historical, with its tripartite division of future, present, and past; and the literary, which is more instinctive— he can think of no conceivable reader for his diary but he still writes it.

What first comes out on the page is the date: it is April 4th, 1984, though we've been told he can't be sure that "this *was* 1984." Next, there is a paragraph giving an account of his previous evening at the flicks: the crass patriotic hysteria of the audience and its amusement at the cruel bombing of a shipload of enemy war refugees, an amusement which is interrupted by the protests of an indignant prole woman. Winston's mind then goes back to the Two Minutes Hate ceremony earlier that morning; but when he turns his attention to the diary again he finds that he has written, no longer in his usual "small but childish handwriting" but in large and voluptuous printed capitals, half a page of "DOWN WITH BIG BROTHER."

When he sees what he has written Winston is tempted to tear the page out of the book in terror; but then he reflects that "the Thought Police would get him just the same," whatever he wrote in the diary, or, indeed, whether he wrote in it or not. Next he writes down, in "a hurried untidy scrawl," the words: "theyll shoot me i dont care theyll shoot me in the back of the neck i dont care down with big brother they always shoot you in the back of the neck i dont care down with big brother." What dooms him, he believes, is that, whether he writes down his thoughts or not, he has in any case committed "the essential crime that contained all others in itself. Thoughtcrime they called it."

The essence of Winston's thoughtcrime can be described by saying that he finds nothing in the life of the present that he can bear, and so his sensibility is dominated by the great question: Were things really better now? Some time later he thinks he may get some help on this from a very old man in a pub for the proles, but finds himself defeated by the random but invincible concreteness of what the old man remembers. Yes, the old man says, beer was cheaper in the old days, and it came in pints. Winston attempts to get him to say more; he lists all the alleged horrors of life in the old days, but he gets no reaction until he mentions the top hats worn by the capitalists, and then the old man recalls the last time he himself had worn a rented top hat, for his sister-in-law's funeral some fifty years ago. Winston goes on with his leading questions until he realizes that "the old man's memory was nothing but a rubbish heap of details," and that he can therefore expect no outside help in his quest to discover whether life was or was not "better before the Revolution than it is now."

He realizes, too, that there is a real urgency in his question, for, in "twenty years, at the most ... the huge and simple question ... would have ceased once and for all to be answerable" because all the evidence would by then have been altered or suppressed. Winston himself works at the Ministry of Truth doctoring the records whenever there has been a change in policy, or some individual has been disgraced or become an "unperson." For instance, we see him having to remove all mention of a formerly prominent member of the Inner Party, Comrade Withers; and in his place he creates, out of whole cloth, a heroic Comrade Ogilvy in "a few lines of print and a couple of photographs." How can there be history when everything inconsistent with the political needs of the Party today has been sent down the "memory hole," and no book exists in Oceania older than 1960? Even worse, something else is disappearing—the sense that merely knowing the true answer is important. For instance, there is the question of the truth or falsehood of the fact that only four years before Oceania had been at war not with its present enemy, Eurasia, but with its present ally, Eastasia; but this question did not seem important even to his love, Julia. Winston does not feel any temptation to tell lies to Julia, but her love for him is based not on her sense of truth, but on her partisan sense that "I knew you were against them"—the Party. Truth itself is already a casualty as far as other people are concerned; and so Winston is forced to accept the terrible conclusion, "History has stopped. Nothing exists except an endless present in which the Party is always right."

As he listens on the canteen television to the statistics of endless claims of increased productivity, Winston compares their picture of how "year by year and minute by minute, everybody and everything was whizzing rapidly upwards" with the disgusting and degrading realities of actual existence. Could he be *"alone* in the possession of a memory?" he wonders. On the other hand, he cannot see how he should feel the present to be so intolerable "unless one had some kind of ancestral memory that things had once been different."

That mute conviction that he is right is one reason for Winston's love of Oldspeak. Newspeak, he senses, in effect creates a conspiracy of silence about all the horrors of the life that he sees going on around him; it epitomizes, to quote Emmanuel Goldstein's book, *The Theory and Practice of Oligarchical Collectivism*, that "denial of reality which is the special feature of INGSOC and its rival systems of thought." The denial is not accidental but systematic. For instance, "The empirical method of thought, on which all the scientific achievements of the past were founded," is totally opposed, Goldstein writes, to the most fundamental principles of Ingsoc.

As a result, he notes, "in Newspeak there is no word for 'Science'."

Winston's friend Syme, who is working in the research department of the ministry on the eleventh edition of the Newspeak dictionary, sees that Winston lacks a real appreciation of Newspeak, "whose whole aim," he says, is to "narrow the range of thought" that the language permits. When the process has been completed, and "Newspeak is Ingsoc and Ingsoc is Newspeak," thoughtcrime will become "literally impossible." Indeed, in the final revision of Newspeak its vocabulary will have been so drastically controlled and reduced in size that "there will *be* no thought, as we understand it now. Orthodoxy means not thinking—not needing to think. Orthodoxy is unconsciousness."

Syme, Winston realizes, will be "vaporized" because he "sees too clearly and speaks too plainly." Winston is soon proved right in his unspoken prediction; but Syme is also right when he says that Winston Smith in his heart would "prefer to stick to Oldspeak, with all its vagueness and its useless shades of meaning." Winston, of course, here exhibits the preference of the writer to that of the politician: and that opposition is fundamental. For, as Syme says, with the final triumph of Newspeak, "the whole literature of the past will have been destroyed. Chaucer, Shakespeare, Milton, Byron—they' ll exist only in Newspeak versions, not merely changed into something different, but actually changed into something contradictory of what they used to be."

The novel does not give us much evidence of Winston's tastes in reading—if only because books of literature, as opposed to pornography and the like turned out collectively by the Fiction Department of the Ministry of Truth, do not seem to exist in the world of *Nineteen Eighty-Four*. Even Goldstein's book, it transpires, was apparently produced collectively. But we are given a good many indications of Winston's literary sensibility. Thus, when Winston dreams of his mother, thirty years missing and probably dead, he sets her and her passionate love for him in a setting of time and place that is very different from the present. It was, he reflects, a time when tragedy was still possible, a time when "there were still privacy, love, and friendship ... dignity of emotion [and] deep or complex sorrows." Winston also imagines a perfect love encounter, which is set in what he thinks of as "the Golden Country"; it is a symbol of the ancient world of pastoral, and when he suddenly wakes up from the promise of the dream, it is "with the word 'Shakespeare' on his lips." Later he sees the lovely rural setting of his first tryst with Julia as "the Golden Country—almost." Winston's literary sensibility, then, contains the notions both of the tragic and the pastoral genres, and also of Shakespeare; and all three are associated with his notions of death and love.

There are other, and perhaps even more significant, details of Winston's literary tastes in *Nineteen Eighty-Four*. First, there is the diary itself. It is a literary *acte gratuit* of a heroic kind, since endangering his life merely to give an objective testimony to his view of the truth about himself and his time surely bespeaks Winston's deep need for self-expression. Secondly, there is another and almost opposite feature of Winston's sensibility—his characteristic obsession with the folk memories of the past; the most important one is the rhyme "Oranges and lemons, say the bells of St. Clement's, / You owe me three farthings, say the bells of St. Martin's, / When will you pay me? say the bells of Old Bailey, / When I grow rich, say the bells of Shoreditch." Here one attraction is the idea that the genre represents the literature of the proles; another is that this particular rhyme is a due to an imaginative reconstitution of the old churches and customs of London as it had once been.

Lastly, there is the way that Winston's love of the past makes him give a symbolic value to the literature, and even to other more physical mementos of history: there is the physical diary itself, a book with cream-laid paper, such as is no longer made; there is the presumably eighteenth-century print of St. Clement's Dane; there is the vast old mahogany bed in which he and Julia make love; and there is the glass paperweight which he buys from old Mr. Charrington and which, Winston imagines, "was the room he was in, and the coral was Julia's life and his own, fixed in a sort of eternity at the heart of the crystal."

Winston Smith's sensibility, then, can be seen as representing a constellation of special intellectual, aesthetic, and literary values. There is the love of what Newspeak calls *oldthink*, that is, the ideas grouped round the equally outmoded concepts of "objectivity and rationalism" and of old folk rhymes. There is, further, his love of the particular and the detailed in other things. It is this love of the particular that makes Winston remember drawing his wife's attention long ago to the "tufts of loose-strife growing in the cracks of the cliff beneath them" in which "one tuft was of two colors, magenta and brick red, apparently growing on the same root." It is also this love of the particular that causes Winston, just before the Thought Police make their strike, to fall asleep "murmuring 'Sanity is not statistical,' with the feeling that his remark contained in it a profound wisdom."

Behind these aspects of Winston's inner sense of values is the larger idea that individual feeling is the most essential and desirable reality available. It is this idea that leads Winston, at his first and only real meeting with O'Brien until his arrest, to propose his toast, "To the past." The Party has persuaded people that "mere impulses, mere feeling, were of no account"; on the other hand, Winston is loyal to the values of an earlier generation—like his mother, who had assumed that "what mattered were individual relationships, and a completely helpless gesture, an embrace, a tear, a word spoken to a dying man, could have value in itself." It is also the rights of individual feeling which cause Winston to conclude that he must continue on his present course to the end; as he put it, if your "object was not to stay alive but to stay human, what difference did it ultimately make?" After all, he reflects, "They could not alter your feelings; for that matter you could not alter them yourself, even if you wanted to."

JOSEPH ADELSON ON SELF AND MEMORY

We are now so accustomed to political lying, it is so much a part of the climate of politics, that we find it hard to credit its traumatic effect upon Orwell. He went to Spain to fight a good clean fight against the Fascists, as so many other innocents did, and once there found that the Communist forces were far more eager to eliminate their rivals on the left than they were to win the war. The word "eliminate" is to be taken literally here, since the Communists meant to do more than win a political victory; they meant to get rid of their rivals by treachery and murder. That was bad enough. What made it worse for Orwell was his discovery upon returning from Spain that the story was not being told, that the slogans of revolution were being used to conceal a bloodbath directed against the revolution itself, that the liberal and left journals in England were quite deliberately telling their readers a pack of lies, which this audience was quite content to believe.

Confronting this state of affairs—the lies told abroad, the lies told at home—enraged Orwell, and ultimately made him a changed man. (...)

So the Spanish war provided Orwell with a theme which was to inspirit his writing for the rest of his life: the political lie—its origins, its vicissitudes, its functions, its aims, its effects. Some of his most powerful essays examine its consequences for thinking and writing: the famous "Politics and the English Language"[9] and "The Prevention of Literature."[10] In "Writers and Leviathan,"[11] one of the last full-scale essays he wrote—on the relation of politics and writing—one finds, in a seven-page article, fourteen separate references to falsehood or self-deception. Even in his minor writing, the casual newspaper columns, we find him contemplating the lie, and its effects on the mind. Indeed, in one of these brief pieces, he offers some examples of what was later to be called "doublethink." Orwell is obsessed by the lie, and I do not use the term pejoratively, since the obsession is rational. Everywhere he looks, he finds that politics, and especially the high-minded politics of the intellectual, consists of people being lied to, and lying to others, and lying to themselves. As you read through the four magnificent volumes of his essays, journalism, and letters, you watch this calm, sardonic man overcome by exasperation—and perhaps some despair, and perhaps some smoldering rage—as he witnesses the triumph of falsehood in world politics. The obsession recedes only in the very last year of his life, when he was writing *Nineteen Eighty-Four*, and which we will imagine was absorbing all he had left to say on those questions.

Through his preoccupation with the lie, Orwell was led in unwitting prescience to issues which were about to overtake psychology and psychiatry—the idea of the self, and its division into true and false sides. To deceive oneself, or to allow oneself to be deceived, without inner protest, is to divide oneself. In dealing with a divided self, as he does in *Nineteen Eighty-Four*, Orwell was looking ahead to psychologies not yet written. He was also—again I suspect unwittingly—looking back to the birth of modern pyschology, in the latter part of the nineteenth century, when such writers as William James and Pierre Janet were trying to fashion a theory of the self, and a theory of inner division. (...)

When the novel opens, Winston Smith is a soul sick and divided, wrong, inferior, and unhappy, who seeks to be unified, to become right, superior, and happy. In William James's language, he seeks "a process of remedying inner completeness and reducing inner discord."[14] He is in a state of anhedonia, a term James brought to general awareness, and which he defined as "passive joylessness and dreariness, discouragement, dejection, lack of taste and zest and spring."[15] He comes to life through his love for Julia, and then seeks to heal his sickness and inner division through a symbiosis with O' Brien. The faith he seeks eludes him; indeed his very seeking is turned against him, cruelly so, for in asking to be replenished, healed, and unified, he is at the end of his journey emptied and destroyed.

Orwell takes the traditional idea of conversion, as we find it in James, and turns it upside down. In its true religious meaning, conversion is a moment of epiphany, in which grace, insight, and conviction arise from within, unbidden, unforced, miraculous. In the brutal, climactic moments of *Nineteen Eighty-Four*, in the chilling dialogue with Winston, O'Brien uses the term twice, first to tell Winston that Julia has betrayed him, and that she did so quickly. "I have seldom seen anyone come over to us so promptly.... It was a perfect conversion, a textbook case."[16] At another point in the interrogation, O'Brien tells Winston that he is not content "with the most abject submission.... We do not destroy the heretic because he resists us; so long as he resists us, we never destroy him. We convert him; we capture his inner mind; we reshape him. We burn all evil and all illusion out of him; we bring him over to our side, not in appearance, but genuinely, heart and soul."[17] You may want to remember James's words on the outcome of conversion—"To be regenerated, to receive grace, to experience religion, to gain an assurance"—and then listen to O'Brien's counterpoint. "Never again will you be capable of love, of friendship, or joy of living, or laughter, or curiosity, or integrity. You will be hollow. We shall squeeze you empty, and we shall fill you with ourselves."[18] Throughout these terrible passages Orwell plays brilliantly upon traditional religious language. O'Brien tells Winston that "everyone is washed clean," and at another point, "always we shall have the heretic at our mercy, screaming with pain, broken up, contemptible— and in the end utterly penitent, saved from himself, crawling to our feet of his own accord."[19]

The destruction of personality O'Brien proposes, undertakes, and achieves has already been prepared by the erosion of personal identity in Oceania, an erosion accomplished by the steady chipping away of memory by its institutions, by doublethink and the memory hole and the Ministry of Truth. The questions which had been nagging at Orwell since his return from Spain, as he witnessed the unchecked spread of deceit in politics, are at last answered in *Nineteen Eighty-Four*: to lie, to be lied to, to accept being lied to, or to rationalize and defend lying for the sake of a better world—all of that, taken to its extreme, will produce a sick and divided soul. The rewriting of history destroys any sense of the past, and with it the sense of personal continuity. That is by no means a surreptitious theme in *Nineteen Eighty-Four*. At the thematic climax of the book, O'Brien asks Winston whether he believes that the past has real existence. He replies that it does, that it can be found in the records, in the mind, and in human memories. O' Brien counters that the Party controls all records and all memories, indeed controls the nature of reality, and to drive the point home undertakes the torture of Winston, forcing him to confess to a false reality, that two and two equal five.

Winston yields, but he has already been weakened, as we learn from his struggle throughout the book to remember his own past. From beginning to end, *Nineteen Eighty-Four* is taken up with Winston's efforts at recollection. At the beginning, "He tried to squeeze out some childhood memory that should tell him whether London had always been quite like this."[20] We soon learn that he has bought a diary, so as to preserve a record of the past for the future, and he fills it with scattered recollections of his own past. Throughout the book he is tormented by a vain attempt to recover memories of his mother and sister, who had disappeared suddenly and without explanation, and at the end we have Winston recalling, unexpectedly, a happy childhood memory, one of reconciliation with his mother—a memory he dismisses as false, saying to himself, "Some things have happened, others have not happened."[21] If that sentence has a familiar ring to it, it is because it repeats Orwell's bitter complaints about the journalism of the Spanish war, that things happened which were not reported, and things did not happen which were.

Winston Smith's argument is Cartesian: "I remember, therefore I exist." To which O'Brien replies, "I control memory, and therefore your existence." As a number of commentators have pointed out, Winston can be understood as a last remnant of Western individualism, now about to be crushed by the megastate. He believes that he is unique and thus precious in possessing a store of personal memory which defines him, and which cannot be taken away from him. It is a claim O'Brien dismisses contemptuously, telling him that men are malleable, and infinitely so. The debate between them is between two views of human nature, both of which can be said to underlie contemporary liberalism, and which account for much of the confusion and contradiction in current democratic thinking. Winston is a Pelagian, in that he believes man to have an intrinsic moral sense and thus an inherent moral dignity. O' Brien is the ultimate Lockean, believing that man is nothing beyond what the social order chooses to instill. As he tells Winston, "We shall squeeze you empty, and we shall fill you with ourselves."

Notes

9. George Orwell, "Politics and the English Language," *CEJL* 4:127–40.

10. George Orwell, "The Prevention of Literature," *CEJL* 4:59–72.

11. George Orwell, "Writers and Leviathan," *CEJL* 4:407–14.

14. [William] James, *Varieties of Religious Experience* [1902; reprint, New York: Macmillan, 1961)], 150.

15. James, *Varieties of Religious Experience*, 127.

16. George Orwell, *Nineteen Eighty-Four* (New York: Harcourt, Brace, 1949), 214.

17. Orwell, *Nineteen Eighty-Four*, 210.

18. Orwell, *Nineteen Eighty-Four*, 211.

19. Orwell, *Nineteen Eighty-Four*, 221.

20. Orwell, *Nineteen Eighty-Four*, 7.

21. Orwell, *Nineteen Eighty-Four*, 243.

RICHARD W. BAILEY
ON THE USE OF LANGUAGE

At the conclusion of the *Communist Manifesto*, Marx and Engels wrote these famous words: "The proletarians have nothing to lose [in a communistic revolution] but their chains."[2] In *The Road to Wigan Pier*, Orwell echoed that slogan in an appeal to those he called fellow members of "the lower-upper-middle class."

And when the widely separate classes who, necessarily, would form any real Socialist party have fought side by side, they may feel differently about one another. And then perhaps this misery of class-prejudice will fade away, and we of the sinking middle class—the private schoolmaster, the half-starved free-lance journalist, the colonel's spinster daughter with £75 a year, the jobless Cambridge graduate, the ship's officer without a ship, the clerks, the civil servants, the commercial travellers and the thrice-bankrupt drapers in the country towns—may sink without further struggles into the working class where we belong, and probably when we get there it will not be so dreadful as we feared, for, after all, we have nothing to lose but our aitches.[3]

For Orwell, the presence or absence of initial *h* was symbolic of the linguistic gulf that matched the chasm separating the social classes of Great Britain. The feature itself is readily recognizable: Orwell alludes to dialects in which *all* and *hall*, *art* and *heart*, *arm* and *harm* are pronounced the same. Then, as now, these dialects of England were primarily urban and working class, and thus in the opinion of "nearly every Englishman, whatever his origins ... the most despised of all."[4]

In *Nineteen Eighty-Four*, the same linguistic feature separates members of the Party from the proles. The two men arguing about the lottery in the prole district do not speak in the way that Winston's colleagues at the Ministry of Truth do; one says, disputing the claim that a number ending in seven has recently been a winner: "No, it 'as not! Back 'ome I got the 'ole lot of 'em for over two years wrote down on a piece of paper."[5] Similarly, the old man in the pub disparages the conversion to the metric system by saying: "'Ark at 'im! Calls 'isself a barman and don't know what a pint is! Why, a pint's the 'alf of a quart, and there's four quarts to the gallon. 'Ave to teach you the A, B, C next" (p. 75).

Orwell does not dramatize his own views of language variety in the novel; instead, he relies on his readers to see the fatal result of Winston's presumption that prole English is despicable and Oldspeak (or "Standard English") is good. In this and in other matters, too many readers have overlooked the difference between Orwell's ideas and those he assigns to his fictional character. Winston, unlike Orwell, despairs of the proles and accepts the values—including the linguistic values— of the lower-upper-middle class; Orwell struggled against temptations to do so. Hence to assume that Winston provides the reference norm for values in the novel is to misread it badly.

Everyone in Oceania suffers from shortages, misery, and capricious violence. Unlike Party members like Winston, however, the proles respond to these circumstances with benevolence: by helping each other (as in the warning that saves Winston from the falling rocket bomb as he walks through the prole district), by encouraging social life (compare the noisy pub with its conversation and dart game to the Chestnut Tree Cafe where talk is drowned by the raucous telescreen and the game of preference is the solitary solution to chess problems), and by giving birth and nurturing families. Only when Winston and Julia's idyll is on the brink of being shattered does Winston have an inkling of his mistake: "The birds sang, the proles sang, the Party did not sing," he thinks to himself, and then voices to Julia his fatal inference "We are the dead" (p. 182).

In *Nineteen Eighty-Four*, speech varieties are the consequence and not the cause of social divisions. Carelessly insensitive to the signs that language provides, Winston presumes that the thought-policeman disguised as Mr. Charrington is somehow cultivated or an aspirant to linguistic respectability because "his accent [is] less debased than that of the majority of proles" (p. 80). Charrington, of course, speaks like a member of Winston's class because he is a member of Winston's class: he is a Party loyalist laying a trap for the two lovers. When Charrington discards his prole disguise, his "cockney accent" disappears (p. 184) and his true voice, "a thin, cultivated voice" (p. 183), emerges as he pronounces the sentence of death. Charrington's accent is, of course, a fake, of a piece with his pretended stoop, his falsely whitened hair, and his altered facial features. In the world of the novel, the nature of one's English is an inevitable consequence of social class. Charrington adopts the "less debased" English that Winston admires as part of his plot, a stratagem that ultimately succeeds. The possibility of a similar ruse occurs to Winston and Julia when they consider vanishing among the proles by learning "to speak with proletarian accents" (p. 126). Yet attempting such a disguise would be "nonsense"; their speech, they believe, would immediately expose them and their class origins.

Orwell consistently believed that working-class and habitually unemployed people were insensitive or indifferent to the variations in English speech that mark social class while the middle class (and above) responded to even the subtlest linguistic hints of social origin. In *Down and Out in Paris and London*, Orwell reported that his dialect was immediately identified in a shelter for the homeless destitute by a fellow old Etonian; speaking in "an educated, half-drunken voice," the stranger initiated a conversation by saying "An old public school boy, what?"[6] Similarly, in *A Clergyman's Daughter*, her fellow tramps find Dorothy Hare's accent unremarkable: "The tramps and Cockney hop-pickers had not noticed her accent, but the suburban housewives noticed it quickly enough, and it scared them.... The moment they had heard her speak and spotted her for a gentlewoman, the game was up."[7] Given that belief, Orwell suggests that Winston and Julia might hide their origins from the proles but could not hope to conceal their accents from an assiduous thought-policeman. On the same basis, he invites his readers to presume that a reasonably vigilant and lower-upper-middle-class Winston should have identified Mr. Charrington as a linguistic anomaly, not upwardly mobile in his speech but as out of place in the prole district as if he had worn his Party uniform.

Orwell's ideology is not always well served by Orwell's fiction. By giving Winston the very attitudes that he despised, Orwell inadvertently sanctions the interpretation of the novel as his dying cry of despair. Yet Winston is a repellent figure who suffers, in part, because he is caught in the pretense and delusion of the lower-upper-middle class. In his evaluation of the spoken varieties of English—his notion that *h*-less speech is ignorant, brutish, and debased while *h*-full speech is wise, benevolent, and cultivated—Winston tumbles into the trap set for him by the Party. He is blinded to the truth by his uncritical acceptance of the conventional wisdom about the connections between accent and aptitude, dialect and decency.

Orwell's own notions about these connections were quite unlike Winston's. In the manuscript diary he kept through his final illness, he persists in his near-lifelong obsession with linguistic varieties. In the entry for April 17, 1949, he writes of his surprise at hearing, after two years in a Scottish sanitarium, the bray of "upper-class English voices."

> And what voices! A sort of over-fedness, a fatuous self-confidence, a constant bah-bahing of laughter abt nothing, above all a sort of heaviness & richness combined with a fundamental ill-will—people who, one instinctively feels, without even being able to see them, are the enemies of anything intelligent or sensitive or beautiful. No wonder everyone hates us so. (*CEJL* 4:578)

How poignant are these, virtually the last, words Orwell was able to write: the distance between his loyalties and those enemy voices suggested by "one instinctively feels"; the recognition that he is inextricably joined by language to those he despises: "No wonder everyone hates us so."

In considering the future of spoken English varieties, Orwell did not think profoundly or reach any very persuasive conclusions. He arrived at a position, but did not know quite what to do with its consequences. "The deadliest enemy of good English," he wrote in 1944, "is what is called 'standard English'" (*CEJL* 3:43). What he wished to do, of course, was to remove the connection between language and social class, and the following muddled account (written in 1944) of what ought to happen to sever that connection is not much improved upon in *Nineteen Eighty-Four*.

> The third thing that is needed is to remove the class

labels from the English language. It is not desirable that all the local accents should disappear, but there should be a manner of speaking that is definitely national and is not merely (like the accent of B.B.C. announcers) a copy of the mannerisms of the upper classes. This national accent—a modification of cockney, perhaps, or of one of the northern accents—should be taught as a matter of course to all children alike. After that they could, and in some parts of the country probably would, revert to the local accent, but they should be able to speak standard English if they wished to. No one should be "branded on the tongue." (*CEJL* 3:51)

In this proposal, Orwell has done little to change the status quo. All he has accomplished, in fact, is to replace one national and class dialect with another, a synthetic "modification of cockney" or "one of the northern accents." The futility of creating a new national dialect was clear enough to him; "all nationalists," he wrote shortly after making his naive proposal, "consider it a duty to spread their own language to the detriment of rival languages, and among English-speakers this struggle reappears in subtler form as a struggle between dialects" (*CEJL* 3:417).

Although he searched for a way to bridge the gap between social classes and between their varieties of spoken English, Orwell failed to find one. Why should there be "a manner of speaking that is definitely national"? Why should some people "revert to local accents" in some parts of Britain but not in others? If "local accents" remain, is it not inevitable that some people "should be 'branded on the tongue'" as long as some accents are more equal than others? Orwell did not discover the answers to these questions. And neither have his successors.

Notes

2. Karl Marx and Friedrich Engels, *Basic Writings on Politics and Philosophy*, ed. Lewis S. Feuer (Garden City, N.Y.: Anchor Books, 1959), 41.

3. George Orwell, *The Road to Wigan Pier* (New York: Berkley Medallion Books, 1967), 191.

4. George Orwell, *Nineteen Eighty-Four* (New York: Signet, 1962), 72. Subsequent references to the novel are cited parenthetically in the text.

5. Sonia Orwell and Ian Angus, eds., *The Collected Essays, Journalism and Letters of George Orwell*, 4 vols (Harmondsworth, Eng.: Penguin, 1970), 3:44. Subsequent references are contained in the text with the citation *CEJL*.

6. *Down and Out in Paris and London* (New York: Harper and Brothers, 1933), 218.

7. *A Clergyman's Daughter* (New York: Harbrace Paperbound Library, n.d.), 163.

ALEX ZWERDLING ON THE ISOLATION OF THE INDIVIDUAL

This sense of a subterranean, deeply irrational current in public affairs is part of Orwell's legacy. He was not of course alone in detecting its presence and his vision was shaped by the events of his time. In 1939, Peter Drucker published his book *The End of Economic Man: A Study of the New Totalitarianism*, a work Orwell knew well and referred to frequently. Drucker argued that neither the fascist nor Russian communist regime could be understood in rational terms. Their adherents had come to believe in a world ruled by demonic forces from which only a quasi-mystical leader could protect them. In Drucker's words,

It is not in spite of its being contrary to reason and in spite of its rejecting everything of the past without exception, but because of it, that the masses flocked to fascism and Nazism and that they abandoned themselves to Mussolini and Hitler. The sorcerer is a sorcerer because he does supernatural things in a supernatural way unknown to all reasonable tradition and contrary to all laws of logic. And it is a sorcerer able to work powerful miracles that the masses in Europe demand and need to allay their intolerable terror of a world which the demons have reconquered.[10]

The primitive fears and exaltations such a view of the world releases are not calculated or strategic, at least in the minds of the adherents. They relate rather to the deepest level of fantasy, often evoked in nightmare, in which our rational faculties are not in control. In that world nothing is implausible; everything is possible.

"Normal men do not know that everything is possible." This is a sentence from David Rousset's ground-breaking study of the concentration camps, *L'Univers concentrationnaire* (1946) which Hannah Arendt uses as an epigraph in her book *The Origins of Totalitarianism* (1951). Rousset's work, which Orwell also knew well, is one of the first attempts to describe the nightmare world fascism had created in the camps, and it is based on his sense of an unbridgeable gap between the knowledge of the internees and the world of "normal men." For the inmates "have experienced anxiety as an ever present obsession.... They have lived through long years in the fantastic setting of degraded human dignities. They are separated from other people by an experience which it is impossible to communicate."[11] Yet it is precisely in fantasy that the two worlds meet, and this is why Orwell's novel is so heavily reliant on it. Modern political terror is essentially reified nightmare. In Hannah Arendt's words,

> Everything that was done in the camps is known to us from the world of perverse, malignant fantasies. The difficult thing to understand is that, like such fantasies, these gruesome crimes took place in a phantom world, which, however, has materialized, as it were, into a world which is complete with all sensual data of reality but lacks that structure of consequence and responsibility without which reality remains for us a mass of incomprehensible data.[12]

Nineteen Eighty-Four attempts to evoke [a] realm of perverse, malignant fantasy. Its historical roots seem to me to lie as much in the first postwar descriptions of what went on in the concentration camps as in the earlier reports of the Soviet purges, though of course the two are related. But the seedtime of Orwell's novel—the mid-1940s in which he was planning the book and composing the first draft—coincided with the first widespread publicity about just what had happened in Dachau and Buchenwald, in Belsen and Treblinka and Auschwitz. (...)

(...) Hannah Arendt has argued that [the] deliberate isolation of the individual, the shattering of all important connections between people and the resulting atomization of society, is "the psychological basis for total domination." For total loyalty "can be expected only from the completely isolated human being who, without any other social ties to family, friends, comrades, or even mere acquaintances, derives his sense of having a place in the world only from his belonging to a movement, his membership in the party."[19] The intention is to transfer the primal emotion between husband and wife, parent and child, between lovers or intimate friends, over to the state.

In *Nineteen Eighty-Four*, the regime strives to become the heir of the moribund family and systematically appropriates the emotional capital of that institution. Its leader, Big Brother, combines the qualities of disciplinarian father and loyal sibling. Even the invented conspiracy against him is called "the Brotherhood." What Winston Smith at first misses from this world is the sense of maternal protection. He dreams ceaselessly about his mother: "His mother's memory tore at his heart because she had died loving him, when he was too young and selfish to love her in return, and because somehow, he did not remember how, she had sacrificed herself to a conception of loyalty that was private and unalterable" (p. 28). Her love was unconditional and uncoercive, and there are really no substitutes for such affection in the public world Winston inhabits.

His task is to transform this need for maternal sponsorship into one of the emotions licensed by the state. The pressure for him to do just this is relentless, and eventually he succumbs.

His disturbing response to O'Brien's torture is a stage in this process: "For a moment he clung to O'Brien like a baby, curiously comforted by the heavy arm round his shoulders" (p. 207). There are only two characters in the novel who address Winston by his first name—his mother, and O'Brien. Others refer to him as "comrade" or "Smith"; Julia calls him "dear" or "love" but never uses his name; the voice on the telescreen barks "6079 Smith W." Only O' Brien persistently uses the intimate, familiar, endearing form of address associated with childhood. It is not entirely ironic that the building in which Winston Smith is being tortured is called the Ministry of Love. By the last paragraph of the novel, when all his other bonds— including the loving bond to Julia—have been cut, he finally twists the strands of his need for mother, father, sibling, and lover into a single emotion. (...)

Orwell's description of the crowd emotions during the daily Two Minutes Hate sessions and in Hate Week suggest a similar manipulation of group response. These scenes are orgies of sadomasochistic feeling, designed to attach a blocked erotic energy to the central figures in the regime's public fiction: the contest between Big Brother and the hated enemy Goldstein. As Winston comes to understand, "There was a direct intimate connection between chastity and political orthodoxy. For how could the fear, the hatred and the lunatic credulity which the Party needed in its members be kept at the right pitch, except by bottling down some powerful instinct and using it as a driving force? The sex impulse was dangerous to the Party, and the Party had turned it to account" (p. 111). The beastlike roar that emerges from the crowd during Hate Week, or "the deep, slow, rhythmical chant of 'B-B! ... B-B! ... B-B!'" that comes unwilled from their throats as Big Brother's powerful face, with its penetrating gaze and hypnotic eyes, flashes onto the screen (p. 17), are examples of the successful channeling of primal emotions to serve the needs of the state. Orwell was trying to convey the atmosphere of a society in which mass psychology, the systematic study and manipulation of crowd response, had become a major force in public life. "Mass-suggestion," he wrote in 1939, "is a science of the last twenty years, and we do not yet know how successful it will be." It seemed to him conceivable that such forces might alter human nature in fundamental ways. "It may be just as possible to produce a breed of men who do not wish for liberty as to produce a breed of hornless cows" (*CEJL* 1:380–81).

Such speculations about the effect of social and political pressures on the human psyche were a hallmark of the intellectual life of Orwell's time. They were the province of a relatively new field of study called "social psychology" that emerged in the period 1930–50. As its name implies, investigators in this field tried to fuse the insights of individual psychology with those of sociopolitical investigation. These years produced works like Harold Lasswell's *Psychopathology and Politics* (1930), Hadley Cantril's *The Psychology of Social Movements* (1941), Theodore Newcomb's *Personality and Social Change* (1943), Wilhelm Reich's *The Mass Psychology of Fascism* (1933; English trans., 1946), and finally *The Authoritarian Personality* by T. W. Adorno and others (1950). The impetus for such studies grew out of a sense that the separation of psychology, sociology, and politics into relatively independent disciplines was responsible for the failure to understand certain vitally important forces in modern life. Psychoanalytic thinking, at least in the early years of the movement, had focused on the shaping power of one's own family and largely ignored the effect of broader societal forces. Adult political behavior had been treated as unrelated to deep psychic needs, despite the new direction suggested in pioneering works like Le Bon's *The Crowd* (1895) and Freud's *Group Psychology and the Analysis of the Ego* (1921).

People trained to think in such watertight compartments could make no sense of some of the major events of their time, let alone of their own experience. Bruno Bettelheim's explanation of how he came to write *The Informed Heart* suggests that the shock of his imprisonment in Dachau and Buchenwald quickly brought about a revolution in his intellectual assumptions.

I was imprisoned in the camps at about the time when my convictions derived from psychoanalysis were at their height: that the personality shaping influence of the immediate family is all important, and that society in the broader sense is relatively negligible by comparison.... My experience in the camps taught me, almost within days, that I had gone much too far in believing that only changes in man could create changes in society. I had to accept that the environment could, as it were, turn personality upside down, and not just in the small child, but in the mature adult too.[30]

As a result of his own experience and his close observation of other prisoners, he came to understand just how malleable the adult personality could still be when subjected to intense societal pressure. And he concluded that "we should never again be satisfied to see personality change as proceeding independent from the social context."[31]

This way of looking at the problem weights the forces unequally: society is the agent, the psyche merely the reagent. And of course since Bettelheim is studying the behavior of involuntary inmates this makes sense. But not all works of social psychology worked with such a simple notion of cause and effect. *The Authoritarian Personality*, for example, is an attempt to understand the personality forces that favored the voluntary acceptance of fascism. Adorno and his associates were trying to explain why modern dictators often had tremendous popular support. To what elements in the psyche were they appealing? What sort of person would be likely to become an enthusiastic follower of such a leader? They tried to describe and account for the prevalence in modern society of what they called "the *potentially fascistic* individual." Such individuals, they concluded, showed "a general disposition to glorify, to be subservient to and remain uncritical toward authoritative figures of the ingroup and to take an attitude of punishing outgroup figures in the name of some moral authority."[32] The study served to show that such personality characteristics were extremely widespread, that they crossed the boundaries of class, age, and sex, and that they were often unconscious.

In social psychology, the individual psyche becomes a microcosm of society itself and a way of studying public life at the cellular level. The kinds of questions that social psychologists try to answer are attempts to explain sociopolitical behavior by linking it to fundamental human needs and fears. "Can freedom become a burden, too heavy for man to bear, something he tries to escape from?" Erich Fromm asks. "Is there not also, perhaps, besides an innate desire for freedom, an instinctive wish for submission?... Is there a hidden satisfaction in submitting, and what is its essence? What is it that creates in men an insatiable lust for power?"[33]

Any reader of *Nineteen Eighty-Four* will recognize these questions. Orwell was a writer of fiction, not a social psychologist. But his deep interest in totalitarianism led him to think about issues of freedom and submission, power and impotence in similar terms. Winston Smith has many of the characteristics described in some of the works of social psychology written in the decade that produced Orwell's novel. He is of course a rebel on the surface and thinks he is joining a conspiracy to bring down a despotic regime. But Orwell makes it clear that at a deeper level Winston wills his own degradation because of his wish to submit. He knows he will be caught, has no chance of escape, yet deliberately chooses a path that can only lead him to a place where he will be—in his own words— "utterly without power of any kind" (p. 137). And when O' Brien stands revealed not as a fellow conspirator but as an agent of the regime, he says to Winston in words that ring true, "You knew this.... Don't deceive yourself. You did know it—you have always known it" (p. 197).

O'Brien is the instrument of Winston's reformation, the force that will allow him to shed his painful, undesired isolation, the confessor who will understand and save him from himself. Winston reflects that at bottom it did not matter whether O'Brien was a friend or an enemy.... O' Brien was a person who could be talked to. Perhaps he did not want to be loved so much as to be understood.... In some sense that went deeper than friendship, they were intimates" (p. 208). This is why he freely surrenders his last secret, the core of his

73

resistance to the state. When O'Brien asks him "Can you think of a single degradation that has not happened to you?" Winston helpfully answers, "I have not betrayed Julia" (p. 225). He thus initiates the final torture with the cage of rats in which he surrenders that last, final loyalty. "Do it to Julia! Do it to Julia!" he screams, "Not me! Julia!" (p. 236).

Orwell's novel depicts a world in which societal pressure has become so relentless that the isolated individual no longer even wishes to hold out against it. The psychic price is too high. Orwell understood the emotional appeal of Hitler's slogan, "Better an end with horror than a horror without end" (quoted in *CEJL* 2:14). In *Nineteen Eighty-Four* he imagined his way into the mind and heart of an unheroic character whose sense of isolation has become unbearable enough to make him want to get rid of the independent self that is creating it. The forces that can lead to such a surrender are analyzed in Bettelheim's *The Informed Heart*.

> The more absolute the tyranny, the more debilitated the subject, the more tempting to him to "regain" strength by becoming part of the tyranny and thus enjoy its power. In accepting all this one can attain, or reattain, some inner integration through conformity. But the price one must pay is to identify with the tyranny without reservation; in brief, to give up autonomy.[34]

This, one might say, is what happens at the end of *Nineteen Eighty-Four*. Winston's final, agonized surrender is his attempt to follow O'Brien's prescription and promise of relief. If only he will submit completely and merge his will in that of the Party, the intolerable burden of his independence will be lifted.

Notes

10. Peter F. Drucker, *The End of Economic Man: A Study of the New Totalitarianism* (London: William Heinemann, 1939), 79–80.

11. David Rousset, *A World Apart*, trans. Yvonne Moyse and Roger

Senhouse of *L'Univers concentrationnaire* (London: Secker and Warburg, 1951), 109. For Orwell's familiarity with Rousset's work, see his letters to Senhouse, *CEJL* 4:419–21.

12. Hannah Arendt, *The Origins of Totalitarianism*, 2d enl. ed. (London: George Allen and Unwin, 1958), 445.

19. Arendt, *Origins of Totalitarianism*, 323–24.

30. [Bruno] Bettelheim, *The Informed Heart: [The Human Condition in Modern Mass Society* (London: Thames and Hudson, 1961)], 134.

31. Bettelheim, *The Informed Heart*, 37.

32. T. W. Adorno, et al., *The Authoritarian Personality* (New York: Harper and Brothers, 1950), I, 228.

33. [Erich] Fromm, *[The] Fear of Freedom* [(London: Kegan Paul, Trench, Trubner, 1942)], 4. It is worth noting that Fromm's ideas on this subject are highly controversial. For a critique, see John H. Schaar, *Escape from Authority: The Perspectives of Erich Fromm* (New York: Basic Books, 1961).

34. Bettelheim, *The Informed Heart*, 294.

BERNARD CRICK ON THE NOVEL AS SATIRE

Freedom and *truth* are the great and obvious affirmations. Not merely their defense but examples of their use run through all Orwell's writings and the way he led his life, and at the very least *Nineteen Eighty-Four* is a satire of all attempts to justify the unfree and the untrue. Only in this passage are they explicit; elsewhere and throughout they are found in the negation of their negation (the technique of satire). The importance of freedom and truth both in the text and to the author is common ground among critics, but not so the theme of mutuality, mutual trust, sociability, even fraternity. Some critics see Orwell as always an individualist, in a strict liberal or neoconservative sense, or as returning fight at the end, in crisis and under stress, to the individualism that had preceded his socialist writings.[7] But notice that in this passage, far from defending individualism as privacy and autonomy, he looks to a time "when men are different" but also one in which "they do not live alone," and he makes, paradoxically to some, "the age of uniformity" also "the age of solitude." Orwell's individualism was not of a liberal kind but either of a republican (sometimes called "civic humanism") or of a modern socialist kind: a person cannot be truly human except in relationships with others. My uniqueness consists not in my "personality" but in the "identity" by which others recognize my actions: it is a mutual, social process, not solitude.[8] Privacy is important to Orwell, but it depends on political action to preserve it: the whole man must move backward and forward, constantly and easily, between public and private: man must be both citizen and individual. Orwell is closer to Rousseau than to Adam Smith or John Stuart Mill.

The ideals are clear, far clearer than the hope of ever regaining what we could lose. Winston has a panic sense of doom, in which Julia shares, when they embark on their illicit affair, "free love" indeed. He had begun actually writing the illegal diary "in sheer panic, only imperfectly aware of what he was setting down"; just before he was interrupted while writing his first entry, he had been "seized by a kind of hysteria" and scribbled: "theyll shoot me i dont care theyll shoot me in the back of the neck i dont care down with big brother." Even when he writes more calmly, "to the future or to the past," he has no confidence that anyone in the future will read his diary or know freedom, truth, and sociability ever again; and he enters the foreboding words: "*Thoughtcrime does not entail death: thoughtcrime* IS *death.*" Orwell is clearly saying that once one gets into a totalitarian regime there is no way out, no hope through conspiracy or rebellion. This view is far from irrationally pessimistic: the Nazis were only defeated externally by war, and it is unlikely that Orwell would have believed that the death of Stalin meant the end of totalitarianism. "The moral to be drawn from this dangerous nightmare situation," he said in the postpublication press release, "is a simple one: *Don't let it happen. It depends on you.*" Our resistance to totalitarian tendencies will be greater if we fight without illusions, above all with no false belief in the inevitability of progress. The worst could happen. And here Orwell drops prudential calculation, as in effect did Winston Smith.

Implicitly he is saying that a man, to remain human, *must* exercise his freedom; he must rebel, however hopelessly: *"theyll shoot me i dont care."* Winston, often dismissed, or labeled as an antihero, is actually a very brave man: he holds out for truth under torture astonishingly long, though it can do him no good at all—"pointless," says O'Brien.

This part of the satire is specifically antitotalitarian. The autocracies of the past had only demanded passive obedience; ceremonies of occasional conformity were all that was needed for law and order. But Orwell implies that totalitarianism demands *complete* loyalty, no reservations being allowed, and continuous enthusiasm, not just occasional conformity.[9] Hence even to think a heterodox thought is a crime, and life without the Party is impossible: *"Thoughtcrime is death."* But precisely because this is *not* typical of autocracies in general, some of the satire aimed at the power-hungry in general or the Party seen as a savage caricature of all bureaucracies, appears both implausible and diffuse. *Totalitarianism* is both too big and too precise to appear relevant to every jack-in-office. Most bureaucrats "let sleeping dogs lie" rather than prosecute vigorously for "Thoughtcrime." Neither bureaucratization nor totalitarianism are to be commended; but they are different phenomena, and threaten each other. Orwell attacks both, but using the same imagery can be confusing. The two birds are hard to kill with the same stone.

"Thoughtcrime" is not commonly found in autocracies, unless Orwell shifts and blurs the focus of the argument from totalitarian regimes to totalitarian *tendencies* (of which there may be some in quite unlikely places). Matthew 5:28— "Whosoever looketh on a woman to lust after her hath committed adultery with her already in his heart" expresses a kind of Thoughtcrime; and Boy Scouts in Orwell's day took a famous and much-mocked oath to be "clean in *thought*, word and deed" (my italics).[10] This was precisely the aspect of Christian teaching that the humanist in Orwell detested. There is also a conscious parody of the Catholic church in the text, especially in the meeting and ceremony in O'Brien's apartment. We know that Orwell was anti-Catholic in the 1920s and

1930s, and attacked the antisocialist influence of the church in postwar Europe. Yet this direct satire of the Catholic church in *Nineteen Eighty-Four* can blur the focus. The church may have some totalitarian tendencies, but Orwell is *not* saying that it *is* totalitarian: it is self-evidently a very traditional kind of autocracy, but also a very special kind. So the satire of total power moves ambivalently between totalitarianism proper and any autocracy, with the Catholic church singled out for special mention in the latter category. It is as if the configuration of powers in the novel form an isosceles triangle with a small, ill-defined, but tangible base of Catholicism between the two long, strong arms of totalitarianism and bureaucratic autocracy (or "managerialism").

The treatment of the proles involves this ambivalence. The Party is plainly a totalitarian party, but the proles are anomalous; they seem familiar and closer to home. They are not mobilized or put into uniform marching columns, and "no attempt was made to indoctrinate them with the ideology of the party"—precisely what Orwell had argued in essays and book reviews was the mark of totalitarianism. This can only be because their main function in the story is to serve as a satire of what the mass media, poor schools, and the selfishness of the intelligentsia are doing to the actual working class of Orwell's time. "Heavy physical work, the care of home and children, petty quarrels with neighbors, films, football, beer and, above all, gambling, filled up the horizon of their minds." All that was required of them was a "primitive patriotism" so as "to make them accept longer working hours or shorter rations," and "a vast amount of criminality," including prostitution and drug peddling, was allowed among them. Also "in all questions of morals they were allowed to follow their ancestral code. The sexual puritanism of the Party was not imposed upon them." So the devices of political control most practiced are not indoctrination and terror, as the Inner Party controls the Outer Party or as in Orwell's conception of real totalitarian regimes, but degradation and fragmentation: "even when they became discontented, as they sometimes did, their discontent led nowhere, because being without general ideas, they could only focus it on petty specific grievances." "Without general ideas" implies that the intellectuals have deserted the working-class movement for the security of desk jobs (the Outer Party).

Yet there is something more to the proles than a Swiftian satire on confounded hopes for the socialist ideal of proletarian man and Orwell's version of the betrayal of the intellectuals. We are told that "they were beneath suspicion" for, "as the Party slogan put it: 'Proles and animals are free.'" And "the Party taught that the proles were natural inferiors who must be kept in subjection, like animals, by a few simple rules." Sir Victor Pritchett once brilliantly described Orwell as "a man who went native in his own country"; and Orwell himself stated in *The Road to Wigan Pier* that he had been led to live among tramps to see if we treated our own working class as he and his fellows had treated the native inhabitants of Burma. So in part at least the proles are "white niggers," a symbol of colonialism: a caricature of the British working class as if they were Burmans or Indians.

Yet despite their degradation, "the proles had stayed human. They had not become hardened inside." "If there is hope," Winston wrote, "it lies in the proles," and the thought is repeated three times. After all, they were "85 percent of the population of Oceania," reasoned Winston (a figure that is repeated in Goldstein's testimony) and "if only they could somehow become conscious of their own strength.... They needed only to rise up and shake themselves like a horse shaking off flies." "And yet—!" he adds. For he remembered at once how he had heard a tremendous shouting in the street, had thought that the proles were "breaking loose at last," but it was only a fight in a crowd of women over scarce tin saucepans on a market stall. "But if there was hope, it lay in the proles. You had to cling on to that. When you put it in words it sounded reasonable: it was when you looked at the human beings passing you on the street that it became an act of faith." Of course Goldstein's testimony is absolutely confident that the proles will conquer in the end, and it provides the "general ideas" that both Winston and the proles lack; but it was written by the Inner Party. "Is it true, what it says?" asks Winston in the cells of Miniluv. "As description, yes. The programme it sets forth is nonsense," replies O'Brien. "The proletarians will never revolt, not in a thousand years or a million." Yet, as I will argue, we are not meant to believe all that O'Brien says either: he is mad, and I think we are meant to believe more of Goldstein than we at first believe (even if "as in a glass darkly," and through a subsidiary and rather confusing satire of Trotskyist rhetoric). So the text is perfectly unclear and deliberately ambiguous as to whether we are to believe in an inevitable victory of the common people. "It must be so" wrestles with "impossible if things go so far." If one puts such historical questions to a fiction, the answer can only be, as Winston sees when he looks at the proles, "an act of faith." Commentators are being far too literal-minded, treating Oceania as Orwell's working model of the future, to argue whether rebellion is possible in such a regime and therefore whether Orwell (not Smith) had despaired. And some socialists are being very obtuse or humorless to say that Orwell had either broken with socialism or is unforgivably rude to the workers to liken them to animals: he had already said in *Burmese Days* that white administrators treated the natives like animals and had recounted in *The Road to Wigan Pier* that he had been brought up to believe that the working class smell (not that they do smell, as shocked left-wing activists angrily misread or wickedly distort him).

Leaving the empirical question aside, however, as being irresolvable in terms of the dramatic needs of a satirical story, there can be little doubt that the author intends us to take very seriously the noble passage, already quoted, "the proles had stayed human." And this is repeated in the nostalgic passage about the proles: "They remembered a million useless things, a quarrel with a work-mate, a hunt for a lost bicycle pump, the expression on a long dead sister's face, the swirls of dust on a windy morning seventy years ago." Irrespective of whether "the last man in Europe" and humanity in general is destroyed or not, we are asked to honor the human spirit in its freedom and oddity: the proles have not been fully debased. Immediately after reading Goldstein's testimony and immediately before their arrest, Winston has a vision that the "hard and red and coarse" prole woman, singing while she hangs up her washing in the backyard, is "beautiful."

> The future belonged to the proles.... [A]t the least it would be a world of sanity. Where there is equality there can be sanity. Sooner or later it would happen, strength would change into consciousness. The proles were immortal, you could not doubt it when you looked at that valiant figure in the yard.... [T]hey would stay alive against all the odds, like birds, passing on from body to body the vitality which the Party did not share and could not kill.

Hope in the inevitability of rebellion is, of course, immediately dashed. The irony is dark and bitter indeed. But her "vitality, which the Party did not share and yet could not kill," remains. Orwell is not saying that the only things that are good are those that we believe are bound to succeed, a simple utilitarianism shared, in his opinion (and that of others) by both Marxists and market liberals. He is saying both that the spirit of the common people cannot be crushed and that even when individuals are crushed, memory of their spiritedness is good in itself.

Notes

7. Such as George Watson, "Orwell and the Spectrum of European Politics," *Journal of European Studies* I, no. 3 (1971): 191– 97 and Norman Podhoretz, "If Orwell Were Alive Today," *Harper's*, January 1983, pp. 30–37 (with a proper reply from Christopher Hitchens in the following issue). Even Alex Zwerdling, in his balanced and scholarly *Orwell and the Left* (New Haven, Conn.: Yale University Press, 1974), says that "the strongly conservative flavor of [his] belief is unmistakable, and the fact that *Nineteen Eighty-Four* was taken up with such enthusiasm by the right is no accident" (p. 110). But he seems to have an ideal image of socialism and confuses cultural conservatism and skepticism about perfectibility (rather than betterment), typical of English socialism, with political conservatism.

8. Kathleen Nott in her *The Good Want Power* (London: Cape, 1977), argues that "identity ... entails a principle of mutual recognition." And see my *In Defence of Politics*, 2d Pelican ed. (New York: Penguin, 1982), pp. 234–35.

9. He says so quite explicitly in essays such as "The Prevention of Literature," *Collected Essays, Journalism and Letters*, ed. Sonia Orwell and Ian Angus, 4 vols. (New York: Harcourt Brace Jovanovich, 1968), 4:64–65, hereafter cited as *CEJL*; "Writers and Leviathan," *CEJL*, 4:407–10; and in his review of *The Totalitarian Enemy*, by Franz Borkenau, *CEJL*, 2:24–26.

10. Quoted by Jeffrey Meyers, *A Reader's Guide to Orwell* (London: Thames and Hudson, 1975), pp. 178–79.

HUGH KENNER ON LANGUAGE, ART, AND POLITICS

(...) Orwell's "plain style" was a deliberate contrivance, formed in response to Newspeak.... All his mature life—alas, only about ten years—he was a leftist at odds with the official left; *Masses and Mainstream* saw in *Nineteen Eighty-Four* evidence of "a hideous ingenuity in the perversions of a dying capitalism." The official left's rhetoric is notoriously abstract; "incorrect" remains one of its doughtiest terms of abuse, to grade *Darkness at Noon* like a geometry paper. Orwell's, by contrast, was deliberately concrete. "As I write, highly civilized human beings are flying overhead, trying to kill me." Written in 1941, that cannot be bettered as a statement of fact. The official left would have spoken of Fascists. Orwell even went on to call those deadly fliers "kind-hearted, law-abiding men" who were victims of the form their patriotism had taken. Was that any way to talk of Fascist hyenas? Yes, it was the only useful way to talk of them, to negate the way the official left talked of them.

He was alert to all of English literature, from Chaucer to *Ulysses*. A source for the famous trope about some being more equal than others has been found in *Paradise Lost*. He had studied Latin and Greek, and once, when hard up, he advertised his readiness to translate from anything French so long as it was post-1400 A.D. Yet he is identified with an

English prose that sounds monolingual: that seems a codifying of what you' d learn by ear in Wigan. Newspeak, as he defined it in *Nineteen Eighty-Four*, seems to reverse the honesty of all that; War Is Peace, Freedom Is Slavery, two plus two equals five. So he chose a linguistic ground: plain talk versus dishonest. We are dealing now with no language human beings speak, rather with an implied ideal language the credentials of which are moral: a language that cleaves to things, and that has univocal names for them. Cat is cat, dog is dog. That, in Swift's time, had been a philosophers' vision, and Swift had derided, in *Gulliver's Travels*, the philosophers who, since words were but tokens for things, saved breath and ear and wear and tear on the lungs by reducing their discourse to a holding-up of things. Ezra Pound likewise in the 1930s was quoting Confucius, to the effect that you begin ideal government by stabilizing names, calling things by what they are properly called by. In the twentieth century as in the eighteenth, that's the readiest naïve model, word stabilized by thing. It gets invoked by whoever has sensed that words are apt to slide.

Orwell lets it stay tacit, a rhetorical undertow. Examine his famous examples, and you discover an absence of apposite *things*. War is not war the way cat is cat, nor is freedom freedom the way dog is dog. Such abstractions are defined by consensus. A few years ago we found ourselves at "war" on poverty; those of us did, anyhow, who accepted the president's rhetoric. And Orwell's point in *Nineteen Eighty-Four* is precisely that Big Brother's rhetoric exerts pressure on the consensus. As for the sum of two plus two, even that is subject to interpretation. Crick cites Soviet posters that used "two plus two equals five" to help citizens make sense of an aborted five-year plan.

Once we've left behind cat and dog and house and tree, there are seldom "things" to which words can correspond, but you can obtain considerable advantage by acting as if there were. You gain that advantage by employing the plain style, which seems to be announcing, at every phrase, its subjection to the check of experienced and nameable *things*. Orwell, so the prose says, had shot an elephant; Orwell had witnessed a hanging; Orwell at school had been beaten with a riding crop for wetting his bed. The prose says these things so plainly that we believe whatever else it says.

Yet in these respects its statements, as we've seen, have been doubted; and we should next observe that Orwell's two climactic works are frank fictions: *Animal Farm* and *Nineteen Eighty-Four*. In a fiction you address yourself to the wholly unreal as if there were no doubt about it. In *Animal Farm* we're apprised of a convention when we're told of pigs talking to one another. But for the fact that we don't credit pigs with speech, we might be attending to a report of a county-council meeting. (And observe which way the allegory runs; we're not being told that councilors are pigs.)

It is very clarifying to reflect on how, linguistically, fiction can't be told from "fact." Its grammar, syntax, and semantics are identical. So Orwell passed readily to and fro between his two modes, reportage and fiction, which both employ the plain style. The difference is that the fictionality of fiction offers itself for detection. If the fiction speaks political truths, then, it does so by allegory. That is tricky, because it transfers responsibility for what is being said from the writer to the reader. Orwell's wartime BBC acquaintance, William Empson, warned him in 1945 that *Animal Farm* was liable to misinterpretation, and years later provided an object lesson himself when he denied that *Nineteen Eighty-Four* was "about" some future communism. It was "about," Empson insisted, as though the fact should have been obvious, that pit of infamy, the Roman Catholic church. One thing that would have driven Empson to such a length was his need to leave the left unbesmirched by Orwell, also Orwell untainted by any imputation that he'd besmirched the left. And it summoned Orwell's shade to Empson's side to abet the hysteria he was indulging at that moment. Empson was writing about *Paradise Lost*, contemplation of which appeared to unsettle his mind.

Now this is an odd place for the plain style to have taken us: a place where there can be radical disagreement about what is being said. "A close, naked, natural way of speaking," Spratt had written; "positive expressions, clear senses,... thus bringing all things as near to the mathematical plainness as they can." Close, naked, natural, that is terminology to depict a restored Eden, before both Babel and Cicero, when Adam's primal language could not be misunderstood: when words could not possibly say the thing that was not. That was when Adam delved and Eve span, and they had both of them the virtues of merchants and artisans: as it were, Wigan virtues.

But the serpent misled them, no doubt employing the high style, and what their descendants have been discovering is that not even the plain style can effect a return to any simulacrum of paradise. Like any spokesman for political decencies, Orwell desired the Peaceable Kingdom. In *Animal Farm* and *Nineteen Eighty-Four* he showed, speaking in parables, how readily its restoration could go awry. And in his ten years of writing before those two books, he demonstrated that the straight is reflexive if not crooked, that all vision is fabrication, all gain short-term, all simplicity contrived. Yes, he'd have gone on writing if he could have lived; and no, he'd never have subdued the inner contradictions of speaking plainly. These correspond to no defect in Orwell's character. They inhere in the warp of reality, as ineluctably as the fact that the root of two is irrational. Divulging that earned one Greek seer a watery death.

JOAN WEATHERLY ON THE NOVEL'S ENDING

Both his defenders and his detractors have noted Orwell's concern in *1984* with the loss of history and humanism in a totalitarian state.[1] Too little attention has been paid, however, to his concern with the attendant loss of art, a concern placing him in the mainstream of English and European letters.[2] The depth of Orwell's feeling for Western tradition and of his understanding of its relationship to tragedy is reflected in his contrast (1941) between the generation of Wells, which lacked awareness beyond "the contemporary English scene," and the generation of Eliot and Joyce, which rediscovered Europe: "They broke the cultural circle in which England had existed for something like a century. They reestablished contact with Europe, and they brought back the sense of history and the possibility of tragedy. On that basis all subsequent English literature that matters twopence has rested, and the development that Eliot and the others started, back in the closing years of the last war, has not yet run its course."[3] The depth of his understanding linguistic and psycholinguistic bases of poetic language is apparent throughout Orwell's work, most obviously perhaps in the 1940 essay "New Words," in which he emphasizes the importance of shared associations for words, the function of imaginative writing, and the difficulty of verbally expressing inner life, especially dreams: "And even if a psychologist interprets your dream in terms of 'symbols,' he is still going largely by guesswork; for the real quality of the dream is outside the world of words."[4]

Failure to consider fully Orwell's aesthetic interest—particularly in tragedy and in its descendant modern Jungian psychology—has led to two distracting misconceptions about *1984*: defenders such as Irving Howe and Philip Rahv read it primarily as a political message, only secondarily if at all, a work of art, and more recently Daphne Patai has viewed the final despair of the novel as a reflection of Orwell's own unconscious misogyny.[5] Surely Oceania is dominated by masculinity—precisely Orwell's point, else why would he name its tyrant Big Brother and take such pains to dramatize Winston Smith's (and Oceania's) loss of the redeeming feminine archetype associated with tragedy since its Dionysian beginnings; but this is not to say that Orwell himself is a misogynist. Through the relationship in *1984* between history, humanism, and tragic art, Orwell explores the same artistic problems treated by Eliot in "Tradition and the Individual Talent" and by Jung in *Modern Man in Search of a Soul*, but in a post Waste Land where tradition has been annihilated, leaving no fragment of the voice of Tiresias to shore against ruin. This post-Nietzschean world goes so far beyond good and evil (or Yeats' substitute for the classical tragic vision, or existentialism) that the very antinomies needed for becoming, for embracing nothingness, are vanishing with Oldspeak.[6]

Hamlet's and Hieronoymo's feigned madness and Crazy Jane's wisdom are impossible for "doublethinkers" and would, in any case, be lost on an audience that laughs at tragedy. Just as Orwell saw that new words must have old, meaningful associations, so Jung saw that meaning depends on memory to connect past and present: "Today" has meaning only if it stands between "yesterday" and "tomorrow" It is "a process of transition" that forms the link "between past and future."[7]

Irving Howe's claim that literature was "the last thing Orwell cared about" as he composed *1984*, was, of course, directed at early critics who failed to see the organic relationship in the novel among political message, flatness of plot and language, and tone of despair.[8] C. E. Jung's theory of archetypes provides one means of approaching this crucial relationship in the novel between the love story and its language and the resulting tone of its tragic message: through Winston's quest for knowledge, Orwell portrays the plight of the artist as "the last man," a tragedian with no opposites to reconcile and with an official language which by forbidding metaphorical union between concrete and abstract images—as it denies joyful sexual union—obliterates all the traditional symbolic meaning by which Jung says man must live.[9] Winston's fragmentary manuscript and Orwell's complex ending, which includes the Newspeak Appendix, both reflect the entropy resulting when the "reconciliation of opposite and discordant qualities," demanded of tragedy by I. A. Richards and by Nietzsche, is absent.[10] Just as Newspeak denies the possibility of creating a new image from the harmonizing comparison of unlikes, the prohibition of art denies the possibility of catharsis or of Dionysian–Apollonian union; and Marx's dialectical materialism, which hoped for proletarian synthesis, is called into question in terms of Jung's law of psychic compensation which, like classical tragedy, demands balancing of discordant elements.[11]

Using INGSOC as a symbol for totalitarianism and Newspeak as a symbol for INGSOC's totally concrete official language, Orwell dramatizes in *1984* the conquest of Winston's self by Big Brother (his animus) over Big Sister (his anima) through the betrayal of O'Brien (his shadow, which on the deeper archetypal level is inseparable from his animus).[12] On the communal surface level of Oceania, INGSOC and Newspeak (rational and animus-dominated) hold supremacy over old Western Europe and Oldspeak, the great sleeping anima-oriented collective unconscious, comprised mainly of the proles. Patai is exactly right in saying that Winston stands "halfway between the powerless personal feminine and the powerful impersonal masculine."[13] Like John Fowles, whose 1964 words *1984* had already dramatized, Orwell understood that poetry is always "more a nation's anima, its particular mystery, its adytum, than any of the [other] arts."[14] Poetry—all literary art—may be mechanically produced in Oceania, but the persistence of anima shines through in the prole songs, in Ampleforth's rhymes, and in Winston's manuscript. Although he at first comes very near murdering Julia, an embodiment of his anima, Winston Smith, "the last man," still possesses enough vague memory of a feminine archetype to achieve temporary reconciliation of his personal opposites. The animus-dominated state wins over individuals, but Big Brother's victory is complete only when Winston at last submerges the healthy anima archetype of his laughing mother, the creative emotional image in whose quest his art had originated. What O'Brien says of Winston as "last" applies not only to Winston, but also to humanism, to Oldspeak, and to art: "Winston you are the last man. Your kind is extinct; we are the inheritors," and "You are outside history, you are non-existent" (p. 222). To be the "last man" is to be at once the last humanist and the last human being with some sense of the anima and the racial unconscious, the last man with enough memory of Oldspeak—not mere language, but culture in its broadest sense—to create, albeit in broken Newspeak, consciousness out of his submerged self.

The reader's terrible knowledge of the extinction of the diary, the record of Winston's quest for self-knowledge, is relieved only by the paradox of art (the contradiction doublethink both uses and says is nonexistent): we *have read* the diary and we still know something of Oldspeak and its language. Like Winston we know "*how*" and, in addition, on the eve of 1984, we have still enough Oldspeak to imagine "*why*" (pp. 179, 215). But "why" is figurative and impossible in doublethink's materialistic dialectic which denies the meaning (spirit) represented by the word (logos); it is O'Brien, the embodiment of the negative shadow archetype, who convinces Smith that "two and two makes five" and that his questioning of "the underlying motives" of society had led him to doubt his "own sanity" (pp. 215, 239).

In reality, it had been those questionings which restored his personal health, and as O'Brien knows, Winston is dangerous to the state because he might well become what Jung calls the voice of his age. He might very well call up "the spirits of his ancestors," the anima archetype in which his "age is most lacking," and be ready to transmute "personal destiny into the destiny of mankind." Jung's description of this awakened artist "who seizes" on the image his age needs and raises it from deepest unconsciousness "into relation with conscious values" fits Winston Smith (and Orwell) exactly. According to Jung—

> The normal can follow the general trend without injury to himself; but the man who takes to the back streets and alleys because he cannot endure the broad highway will be the first to discover the psychic elements that are waiting to play their part in the life of the collective. Here the artist's relative lack of adaptation turns out to his advantage; it enables him to follow his own yearnings far from the beaten path, and to discover what it is that would meet the unconscious needs of his age. Thus, just as the one-sidedness of the individual's conscious attitude is corrected by reactions from the unconscious, so art represents a process of self-regulation in the life of nations and epochs.[15]

Through the story of his artist figure, Orwell himself fulfills the function of both the historian and the poet as defined by Aristotle: he tells us "what has happened" and "what may happen" through the tragedy of Winston Smith, who is duped by his negative shadow.[16]

Notes

1. Irving Howe, *Politics and the Novel* (New York: Horizon Press, 1957), p. 239. See also Erich Fromm, Afterword, *1984* by George Orwell (1949; rpt. New York: New American Library, 1981), pp. 258, 266–267.

2. From the time Eric Blair took the pen name Orwell (which was perhaps suggested to him by the pleasure Chaucer's Merchant took in the trade connection between the continent and the mouth of the Orwell at Orwelle Haven) until the last days of his life when, in preparing notes for a biography of Joseph Conrad, he complimented the Pole on his European perspective, he never lost sight of the crucial relationship between Britain and the continent. See George Orwell, *The Collected Essays, Journalism and Letters of George Orwell*, ed. Sonia Orwell and Ian Angus (New York: Harcourt, Brace and World, 1968), IV, 489.

3. George Orwell, "The Rediscovery of Europe," in *The Collected Essays, Journalism and Letters of George Orwell*, ed. Sonia Orwell and Ian Angus (New York: Harcourt, Brace and World, 1968) II, 206–207.

4. George Orwell, "New Words," in *The Collected Essays, Journalism and Letters of George Orwell*, ed. Sonia Orwell and Ian Angus (New York: Harcourt, Brace and World, 1968), II, 3–4, 5, 9.

5. Howe, p. 237; Philip Rahv, "The Unfuture of Utopia," *Partisan Review*, 16 (1949), 7; and Daphne Patai, "Gamesmanship and Androcentrism in Orwell's *1984*," *PMLA*, 97 (1982), esp. 866–69. See Richard I. Smyer, *Primal Dream and Primal Crime: Orwell's Development as a Psychological Novelist* (Columbia: University of Missouri Press, 1979), for an interesting Freudian reading of Orwell; see pp. 176–182 for an excellent Bibliography. Richard Rees, *George Orwell: Fugitive from the Camp of Victory* (London: Secker and Warburg, 1961), p. 8, has no recollection of his friend Orwell's mentioning Freud or Jung. There are several references to Freud in Orwell's writings and Bernard Crick, *George Orwell: A Life* (Boston: Little, Brown, 1980), p. 168, reports that Rosalind Obermeyer—the friend and landlady who first introduced George Orwell to his future wife Eileen O' Shaughnessy (who was then completing graduate work in psychology)—was "a psychologist of Jungian persuasion." Aside from these intimate connections with several psychologists, there are striking parallels between Orwell's and Jung's common concerns with the World Community of Modern Man—not to mention such uncanny examples of synchronicity, if nothing else, as their common usage of smelly sinks to depict the plight of Modem Man. Jung's works were available in English translation from 1922 onward and the striking similarities between Orwell and Jung begin appearing years before Orwell met O'Shaughnessy.

6. See Morse Peckham, *Beyond the Tragic Vision* (New York: George

Braziller, 1962), esp. 364–372, for excellent discussion of Nietzsche's view of tragedy; and Friedrich Nietzsche, *The Birth of Tragedy and the Case of Wagner*, trans. Walter Kaufman (1886; rpt. New York: Vintage, 1967), esp. pp. 38–81, for Nietzsche's discussion of the reconciliation of Dionysian and Apollonian in tragedy.

7. C.G. Jung. *Modern Man in Search of a Soul*, trans. W. S. Dell and Cary F. Baynes (1934; rpt. New York: Harcourt Brace, 1934), p. 228.

8. Howe, p. 237.

9. C.G. Jung, *The Archetypes and the Collective Unconscious*, trans. R. F. C. Hull (1936; rpt. Princeton, N.J.: Princeton University Press, 1959), esp. pp. 7, 46–49, 64–66; George Orwell, *1984*, (1949; rpt. New York: New American Library, 1981), p. 222. Cited parenthetically by page number in remainder of text. Orwell had originally planned to call the novel *The Last Man in Europe*.

10. I.A. Richards, *Principles of Literary Criticism* (New York: Harcourt Brace and World, 1925), pp. 245–46.

11. Jung, *Modern Man in Search of a Soul*, p. 241.

12. For an excellent introduction to Jung's concept of archetypes, see Joseph Campbell, Introd., *The Portable Jung*, by C. G. Jung (1971; rpt. New York; Penguin, 1982), pp. xxi–xxxii. See also "Aion: Phenomenology of the Self," pp. 139–162.

13. Patai, p. 866.

14. John Fowles, *The Aristos* (1964; rpt. New York: Plume, 1970), p. 210.

15. C.G. Jung, "On the Relation of Analytical Psychology to Poetry," in *The Portable Jung*, ed. Joseph Campbell, pp. 321–322.

16. Aristotle, *Poetics*, trans. S. H. Butcher (1895; rpt. Great Books Foundation, 1956), Section IX, p. 13.

MICHAEL P. ZUCKERT ON WINSTON'S DEFEAT

Ordinary power is a self-assertion of some sort. But power, as expressed in *1984*, is different in that it is altogether selfless. "The first thing you must realize," O'Brien tells Winston Smith, "is that the individual only has power so long as he ceases to be an individual."[24] Paradoxically, the self must cease being a self in order to successfully assert itself. O'Brien's seemingly contradictory position on the self is a response to the contradictory and necessarily failing character of every particular act of self-seeking.

> Alone—free—the human being is always defeated. It must be so, because every human being is doomed to die, which is the greatest of all failures. But if he can make complete, utter submission, if he can escape from his identity, if he can merge himself in the Party so that he is the Party, then he is all-powerful and immortal.[25]

At the center, then lies the problem of death. Every human act, every assertion and seeking of self and power, is an act aimed at conquering death. Human life and human deeds are expressions, broadly speaking, of the urge to self-preservation, even, we might say, of the urge to establish and maintain a self. Yet every such act is doomed to failure because of the implacable foe, death. Try as hard as they can, evade as far as they can, build walls, build guns, build with love, build with hope-whatever men try, they necessarily fail. The individual dies and with him all his self-assertions.

O'Brien's point is that if men would only be a little more radical in their self-assertions, if they would frankly and entirely recognize what they seek, then their goal can be achieved. If they can lose their individual selves altogether and merge with a collectivity, they can survive; if they are the Party, then they outlive the puny body which houses them in the collective entity which lives on. The paradox of O'Brien's position is that the completely self-assertive person is completely self-effacing. To paraphrase, "he who would find himself, must lose himself."

The human mind can thus conquer death, the greatest limit on man. Power is first and foremost the conquest of death; thus, the Inner Party realizes, to be is to exercise power. The successful exercise of power becomes possible with the realization that mind can conquer not only death but every external reality. Every one of the most interesting features of Oceania expresses the drive of mind to conquer everything external or objective. The subjectivity of the mind claims primacy over everything objective. The principle of the conquest of death is the recognition of the freedom of the mind. The mind, free to redefine or recenter the self, conquers death through the creation of a collective and immortal self. The mind, unlike the body, is free from nature. This discovery is the vehicle for all the other conquests.

We understand the conquest of nature in terms of science and technology, but for Ingsoc this is not the avenue.

[Winston asks:] "But how can you control matter? You don't even control the climate or the law of gravity. And there are disease, pain, death—"

O'Brien silenced him by a movement of the hand. "We control matter because we control the mind. Reality is inside the skull. You will learn by degrees, Winston. There is nothing that we could not do. Invisibility, levitation—anything. I could float off this floor like a soap bubble if I wished to. I do not wish to, because the Party does not wish it. You must get rid of those nineteenth-century ideas about the laws of nature. We make the laws of nature."[26]

Reality is altogether, or for all practical purposes, in the mind: this radical principle also lies behind the conquest of history, that part of Oceania with which Winston, and thus the reader, had special connection, through his job at the Ministry of Truth. In Oceania, history is what the rulers say it is, and it can change from day to day, for the rulers are able to control the pieces out of which history is constructed. No man by himself can establish and authenticate reality, even a reality he has himself experienced. The world, Orwell sees, is intersubjective. Only social authentication makes belief possible. The individual memory lacks sufficient confidence in itself to stand against the testimony of the "documents" and the "others," which the Party has the power to manipulate. The "objective reality" of the past is really quite irrelevant in Oceania, for the truth is always mediated through human consciousness, and the principles which determine human consciousness are quite other than truth.

Even though Winston has been part of the machinery which established historical "reality," according to the principles of Ingsoc, he nonetheless recoils from O'Brien's revelations.

> The belief that nothing exists outside your own mind—surely there must be some way of demonstrating that it was false. Had it not been exposed long ago as a fallacy? There was even a name for it, which he had forgotten.[27]

Of course Winston is searching for "solipsism," but O'Brien quickly corrects him: "You are mistaken, this is not solipsism. Collective solipsism, if you like. But that is a different thing; in fact, the opposite thing."[28] It is "the opposite thing" because "solipsism" is the thesis that the individual consciousness defines reality for itself; Ingsoc's "collective solipsism" depends on recognizing the inability of the individual consciousness to define reality for itself, and the individual's dependence on collective or social consciousness. Ingsoc's collective solipsism plays out the modern skepticism regarding the human mind's directness of access to the phenomena of the world: the mind knows ideas, or constructs; it does not know "the things themselves."[29] Orwell grasps well the subjectivist character of modern thought, and he extrapolates from his own experience of intersubjective or socially determined consciousness which the history of his times showed on a large scale. A common theme of Orwell's work, going at least as far back as "Shooting the Elephant," is the power of the social whole over the individual mind. Orwell's fixation with "telling the truth" and standing against the crowd, are the response of a man who personally felt the power of the crowd over his own mind. "Confessions" at purge trials, the brazen rewriting of history, inducing conviction in the minds of men by sufficient repetition and control of what can and cannot be said and validated in public spaces-these broader historical experiences of his time must have convinced Orwell that the power of collective solipsism was great indeed.

Notes

* This paper was originally prepared as part of a program on Orwell's *1984*, sponsored by the Minnesota Humanities Commission. An earlier version was first delivered as part of a symposium at Shattuck-St. Mary's Schools, Fairbault, Minnesota, Spring 1984.

24. [George] Orwell, *1984* [(New York: Harcourt Brace Jovanovich, 1977)], p. 267.

25. Ibid.

26. Ibid., p. 268.

27. Ibid., p. 269. On the issue of modern subjectivism, one must consider above all the work of Martin Heidegger, e.g., his *Nietzsche*, David F. Krell, editor (San Francisco: Harper & Row, 1982), pp. 96–139.

28. Orwell, *1984*, p. 269.

29. Compare Christopher Small's critique of O'Brien's position in *The Road to Miniluv*, p. 155. Small misses the collective character of the solipsism here, and thus mistakenly believes he can readily refute O' Brien on solipsistic grounds.

MICHAEL SHELDEN ON AUTOBIOGRAPHY AND THE NOVEL

[*Nineteen Eighty-Four*] is Orwell's most compelling work, and its enormous success over the years is well deserved, but it is also his most misunderstood work. Endless theories have been put forward to explain its vision of the future, but not many critics have been willing to see how firmly rooted it is in Orwell's past. Almost every aspect of Orwell's life is in some way represented in the book. Winston Smith's yearning for the green wilderness of the 'Golden Country' is very much connected to Orwell's long-standing affection for the lost Edwardian world of his childhood in Henley. The objects of that older world have been discarded as 'junk' in Big Brother's world, but Winston tries to hold onto a few pieces of this 'junk' as a way of maintaining his links with the past. In a similar way Orwell spent a good deal of time in the 1940s, while he was living in London, haunting junk shops with mountains of old, apparently useless items from another age. Just as Winston finds a beautiful paperweight in an old shop and clings to it as though it were a kind of life preserver, so Orwell praised junk shops in the *Evening Standard* in 1946—celebrating the joys of 'useless' relics from a time long before Hitler and Stalin and atom bombs. He specifically mentioned his delight at discovering 'glass paperweights with pictures at the bottom. There are others that have a piece of coral enclosed in the glass.' ... Winston's, of course, has a piece of coral embedded in it, and he examines it intently, surprised that anything so delicate could survive in a brutal age.

Orwell's experience of bullying at St Cyprian's cannot be discounted as an influence on *Nineteen Eighty-Four*. He was working on 'Such, Such Were the Joys' when he was in the early stages of writing the novel, and there is an overlapping of theme between the two works. Both are concerned with the ways in which people can be manipulated to look up to their tormentors as superior beings who should be respected—even loved—rather than as the objects of the hate which they have earned. Young Eric Blair was made to feel guilty because he did not love Mrs Wilkes, and he took comfort in knowing that, in his heart of hearts, he felt only hatred for her. Likewise, Winston must struggle against the temptation to love Big Brother, fighting back the desire to surrender his hatred in the face of overwhelming power. He feels just as helpless against such power as young Eric felt in the face of Mrs Wilkes's authority.

For models of authoritarian power at work Orwell could look to incidents from his life in the Indian Imperial Police, his experiences in Barcelona when the government was trying to suppress the POUM, and his encounters with the absurdities of wartime censorship—at the BBC as well as in his ordinary work as a journalist. It is not the case, by any means, that these relatively mild forms of tyranny are worthy of any close comparison with Big Brother's nightmarish rule, but all of these elements helped to give Orwell a certain feel for the life which he describes in the novel, a life which is ultimately the work of his imagination, but which is based on real experience. When he describes torture in the novel, for example, he is able to draw on his memories of milder forms of torture—both mental and physical—at St Cyprian's, and in Burma. And when he describes the mindless, never-ending warfare, with bombs exploding randomly every day, he had only to recall the sensations he felt during the Blitz, and later during the attacks from Hitler's V-1 flying bombs and V-2 rockets. The cold, drab environment—with its scarcities and bad food—is partly a reflection of conditions in Britain during much of the 1940s.

Stephen Ingle on Historical Roots

If Orwell wanted to get this message across to socialists generally it was no wonder that he attracted the opprobrium of a number of socialist intellectuals: indeed *Nineteen Eighty-four* was reviewed in one communist journal under the heading 'Maggot of the month', and the reaction of the radical student in Saul Bellow's *Mr Sammler's Planet* indicates that he had not been forgiven more than twenty years later. 'Orwell was a fink,' he says. 'He was a sick counter-revolutionary. It was good he died when he did.' Even such a perceptive critic as the socialist intellectual Raymond Williams could not forgive Orwell's attacking totalitarianism through the example of *socialist* totalitarianism (or indeed revolution through the example of a socialist revolution).[24] It would have been easy enough for Orwell to have avoided these charges had he wanted to, but the point is precisely that he was writing to praise and not to bury socialism! His readers, or more correctly those for whom he was writing, did not need to be told that fascism was by its nature totalitarian; had not a world war just been fought for this very reason? They did not need to be told that many foreign regimes with an authoritarian disposition could easily slip into totalitarian ways; had not pre-war history shown that all too clearly? But what the insular British left *did* need to be told was that totalitarianism could be built by a socialist regime and that even Britain, with its long and distinguished tradition of liberal values, could provide the home for a totalitarian polity. Orwell wrote *Nineteen Eighty-four* within the British socialist tradition to warn fellow socialists to be on their guard against an intellectual elite which he despised and which he believed to be chiefly interested in power for its own sake.

The ruling class in *Nineteen Eighty-four* established itself in Oceania as the consequence of a socialist revolution and it founded a socialist state which presented itself as an organic whole, subsuming the individual interests of all. But this organicism is soon exposed, for society is organised, indeed regimented, solely for the purpose of maximising the self-interest of the ruling group. It is a perversion of Plato's republic, with power (as defined in *Miss Blandish*) and not virtue as the rulers' reward. Technology, applied specifically to the science of scrutiny, provides the means for the group's dominance, but the superstructure which it supports assigns a social role to groups with a rigidity unimaginable even in feudal Christendom. Thus Oceanic society comprises 300 million of whom party members make up 45 million (fifteen per cent); of these, six million (two per cent of the whole) belong to the Inner Party and thirty-nine million (the remaining thirteen per cent) to the Outer Party. The eighty-five per cent of the population who do not belong to the Party comprise the proletariat and are not, in the classical sense, citizens of the state at all.

The purpose of this rigid hierarchy is not immediately apparent and the novel's hero, Winston Smith, wrote in his diary that although he understood *how* the Inner Party retained its control of the state he did not understand *why*; it was clearly no longer motivated by socialist ideology. The purpose of the hierarchy was finally explained to Winston by his interrogator O'Brien as being simple—power. O'Brien defines power not as a means to obtain some end (equality or justice for example) but an end in itself. He argues that no group ever seizes power with the intention of giving it up later. Dictatorships are not set up in order to defend the revolution; rather the revolution is organised to set up a dictatorship. Power is not a means, it is an end.[25] O'Brien goes on to define power: power is being exercised when one individual forces his or her own view of reality upon another, and in a most specific way.[26]

> 'How does one man assert his power over another Winston?'
> Winston thought. 'By making him suffer', he said.
> 'Exactly. By making him suffer. Obedience is not enough. Unless he is suffering, how can you be sure that he is obeying your will and not his own? Power is in inflicting pain and humiliation. Power is in tearing human minds to pieces and putting them together again in shapes of your own choosing.'

The future, O'Brien explains to Winston, consists of the members of the Inner Party maximising power through their relationship with the Outer Party. 'If you want a picture of the future,' says O'Brien, borrowing from James Hadley Chase, 'imagine a boot stamping on a human face forever.'

This constitutes a theory of power as psychosis, arguing that those who seek political power do so simply to inflict suffering on others. Moreover in order to maximise the satisfaction which the exercise of power brings, it has to be exercised directly. On this basis a playground bully might be said to exercise greater power than a president of the United States, since the satisfactions of inflicting suffering are more immediate and direct. Can it seriously be maintained that the majority who have sought and exercised power throughout history have been motivated by no considerations other than stamping on faces? George Kateb feels that Orwell's linking of power with sadism is unsound and diminishes the strength of his warning.[27] Hannah Arendt[28] has emphasised that all ideological thinking contains elements of totalitarianism because, by definition, they provide total explanations of 'the truth'. Moreover, since totalitarian leaders declare the nature of ideology *ex cathedra*, ideology may be cynically used to sanction the pursuit of total power. This is precisely the argument that Burnham advances in *The Machiavellians* and, indeed, is similar to Popper's thesis that ideology is a means and not an end.[29] It would seem, then, that Orwell is in very good company when he links ideology with power, but not when he links both to sadism.

Perhaps what Orwell had in mind was to parody power; to show us that those who wish to create power structures, especially of a totalitarian nature, in order to create a better world for all, such as the Fabians, were concerned just as much with forcing their reality upon others, concerned just as much with creating, using and benefiting from that power structure, which they would be unwilling ever to dismantle. Isaac Deutscher argued that Orwell's 'ferocious imagination', because it lacks the subtleness and originality of the greatest satirists, leads him to overstate his case. Nevertheless his analysis is both penetrating and arresting.[30]

It would probably suit Orwell's purpose well enough if he could frighten us into understanding two things: that power is an end just as much as a means and that totalitarianism is not rational. Ironically it was the one-time Fabian H. G. Wells himself who warned against allowing a man to appoint himself as your shepherd, for sooner or later you would find a crook around your ankle. As for the second, Orwell clearly regarded it as important to explore the associated myth of totalitarian rationality. He criticises H. G. Wells for depicting history as a struggle between science and planning on the one hand and disorderly reaction on the other. The truth of the matter was quite a different thing: 'The order, the planning, the state encouragement of science, the steel, the concrete, the aeroplanes, all are there, but all in the service of ideas appropriate to the Stone Age. Science is fighting on the side of superstition.'[31] Again, power, shown to be atavistic and irrational, is the *end*, and scientific rationality only a *means*.

The new social order of Oceania in which all pretence is stripped away allows the Inner Party to maximise power, its sadistic satisfaction gained through the suffering of others. Orwell wrote that former civilisations claimed to be founded on love or justice; the Party's order is founded on hatred. In both the old classical theories of the state and that of Oceania, private property and family life have been abolished so that nothing may come between the guardian (Inner Party member) and the state; in Oceania, moreover, all forms of passion not channelled through—indeed directed by—the state are illegal. Orwell says that family life will cease to exist at all in the future, just as in Huxley's *Brave New World*. But whereas with Huxley the power of the sex is diffused, with Orwell it is eradicated: 'We shall abolish the orgasm.... [T]here will be no loyalty except loyalty to the party.'[32]

It was against this ruling group that Winston pitched himself. He had come to regard himself as the guardian of human values and he sought to maintain these values while recognising from the beginning the inevitability of his eventual defeat. Winston acted against the state by trying to create a private realm—through purchasing and keeping a diary and by indulging in a love affair. He also declared his willingness to act against the state politically. When O'Brien, posing as a leader of the clandestine rebels, the Brotherhood, asked Winston what acts he would be prepared to undertake against the state, Winston agreed to do anything, however devastating its effects upon innocent people. A more crucial point, however, is that Winston's treachery predated this declaration of intent, predated even the purchase of the diary; to question the infallibility of the state within the confines of one's skull was to be doomed— thoughtcrime was treachery. In much the same way that Koestler's Rubashov, in *Darkness at Noon*, nightly expected a visit from the secret police once he began to question the propriety of Number One's policies within the privacy of his own skull, so too Winston knew where his thoughtcrimes would inevitably lead. This lack of a distinction between a private and a public realm is precisely what gives life in Oceania its nightmare quality. Nobody has recourse to a private world in which he or she may regain self-esteem or attempt to control even the smallest part of their own destiny; there is no escape from Big Brother.

What are the elements of the private realm, denied by the Oceanian state, which allow an individual to be fully human? First, the right to be one's own judge of external reality, to be what Arendt calls a 'moral man'.[33] In essence it was what

Martin Luther sought to establish by claiming to have direct access, as it were, to God, and not to require the mediation of the Church. The Party stands firmly against this claim, demanding that the individual be willing to reject the evidence of his or her own senses. Reality is not external, says O' Brien, It is the creation of the human mind. Not the individual mind, which makes mistakes and is mortal, but in the mind of the Party, which is collective and immortal. Whatever the Party holds to be truth is truth. It is impossible to see reality except by looking through the eyes of the party. It was also impossible to guess what the party might declare to be reality at some time in the future. Winston conjectures that in the end the Party would declare that two plus two made five and the individual would be required to *believe* it (to *accept* it would not be sufficient). 'It was inevitable that they should make that claim sooner or later: the logic of their position demanded it.' Indeed, when reviewing Bertrand Russell's *Power: A New Social Analysis* in 1939, Orwell had predicted an age 'in which two and two will make five when the Leader says so'.[34] Orwell drew his inspiration here from Eugene Lyons who, when writing about his experiences in the Soviet Union, had noted that when the targets of Five Year Plans were allegedly achieved in four years, adverts were put up in neon in Moscow reading: '2 + 2 = 5' . For Lyons these signs, with what Steinhof calls their mystical simplicity, defiance of logic and 'nose-thumbing arithmetic' came to epitomise the Soviet system.[35] For his part Winston was brought to such a poor condition physically that he was genuinely no longer certain whether, when O'Brien added two fingers to two, he could see four or five. It is important to appreciate what it is that Winston is claiming: that 'the truth' constitutes an objective reality which is accessible to the undeceived intelligence on the basis presumably of sensory witness.

Notes

24. Raymond Williams, *Orwell*, Fontana, 1971.

25. *Nineteen Eighty-four*, Penguin, 1960, p. 211.

26. Ibid., p. 214.

27. George Kateb, 'The Road to Nineteen Eighty-four', *Political Science Quarterly* 4, 1966, pp. 565–81.

28. Hannah Arendt, *The Origins of Totalitarianism*, Harcourt Brace Jovanovich, 1973.

29. Karl Popper, *The Open Society and its Enemies*, 2, Routledge, 1968.

30. Isaac Deutscher, 'The Mysticism of Cruelty', in *Heretics and Renegades*, Hamish Hamilton, 1955.

31. 'Wells, Hitler and the world state', *CEJL* 2, pp. 139–45.

32. Ibid., pp. 214–5.

33. Arendt, *1973*, p. 451.

34. *CEJL* 1, pp, 375–6.

35. William Steinhof, *Road to Nineteen Eighty-four*, Weidenfeld and Nicolson, 1975, p. 172.

Works by George Orwell

"Awake Young Men of England" (poem), 1914.

"The Spike" (essay), 1931.

"The Hanging" (essay), 1931.

Down and Out in Paris and London, 1933.

Burmese Days, 1934.

A Clergyman's Daughter, 1935.

Keep the Aspidistra Flying, 1936.

The Road to Wigan Pier, 1937.

Homage to Catalonia, 1938.

Coming Up for Air, 1939.

"Inside the Whale" and Other Essays, 1940.

The Lion and the Unicorn: Socialism and the English Genius, 1941.

Animal Farm: A Fairy Story, 1945.

Critical Essays: Dickens, Dali, and Others, 1946.

Such, Such Were the Joys (essay), 1947.

1984, 1949.

"Shooting an Elephant" and Other Essays, 1950.

"England, Your England" and Other Essays, 1953.

Collected Essays, 1961.

Orwell's published work includes many shorter pieces published in *Adelphi, Time and Tide, Tribune, The Observer, Partisan Review*, and *The Manchester Evening News*.

Annotated Bibliography

Crick, Bernard. *George Orwell: A Life*. London: Secker & Warburg, 1980.

Crick's work was originally commissioned by Sonia Orwell, but after seeing the result she withdrew the commission. Crick published the book regardless, producing what is generally regarded as a dry, almost statistical account of the writer's life that is focused solely on the development of political ideas.

Davison, Peter. *George Orwell: A Literary Life*. New York: St. Martin's Press, 1996.

Davison edited the nine-volume *Complete Works of George Orwell,* and by doing so he learned much regarding the works that had influenced the author, as well as Orwell's relationships with editors and how they affected his work. As a result, Davison's concern in *A Literary Life* is with the literary influences that can be felt in Orwell's work.

Hammond, J.R. *A George Orwell Chronology*. Hampshire: Palgrave, 2000.

Hammond's chronology provides a useful quick-reference chronology of Orwell's life.

Hitchens, Christopher. *Orwell's Victory*. London: Allen Lane, 2002.

Hitchens argues zealously that Orwell was a progenitor of current leftist thinking on postcolonialism and socialism; *The Guardian* and *The London Review of Books* both reviewed the book and judged that it oversimplifies a complex individual.

Howe, Irving, ed. 1984 *Revisited: Totalitarianism in Our Century*. New York: Harper & Row, 1983.

An influential collection of essays published as a consequence of a conference, held on the verge of Orwell's prophetic date, that gathered leading Orwell scholars to consider his novel in a historical and more broadly cultural light.

Meyers, Jeffrey. *Orwell: Wintry Conscience of a Generation*. New York: W.W. Norton, 2000.

Meyers engages Orwell through newly considered material—unpublished correspondence and the like from the Orwell Archive in London—and approaches the author's human character, the contradictions between his ideas and his actions, his relationships with women, and his childhood feelings of inferiority. Richard Bernstein, in a *New York Times* review of the book, praised Meyers' thoroughness in exploring Orwell's sense of guilt and its effect on Orwell's art.

Patai, Daphne. *The Orwell Mystique: A Study in Male Ideology*. Amherst: University of Massachusetts Press, 1984.

Patai's book, the first large-scale feminist study of Orwell's work, has been cited often by a range of subsequent scholars.

Savage, Robert, James Combs, and Dan Nimmo, eds. *The Orwellian Moment: Hindsight and Foresight in the Post-1984 World*. Fayetteville: University of Arkansas Press, 1989.

This collection of essays blends views from scholars in political science, futurist studies, linguistics, and literary criticism in an attempt to apply Orwell's ideas (as they appear in his text) to contemporary situations.

Shelden, Michael. *Orwell: The Authorised Biography*. London: Heinemann, 1991.

At the time of its publication, this book was widely regarded as the most thorough account of Orwell's life. Shelden's biography was written with total access to Orwell's papers, family, friends, and associates, as well as some narrative flair. Shelden's text benefited from better access than his predecessors Stansky and Abrahams had had, better prose and narrative ability than Crick, and a more ambitious scope than Davison. Still, mixed reviews of the book accused

Shelden of providing no insight into Orwell's personal life; either Orwell was a man of entirely superficial attributes, they opined, or Shelden could have provided deeper analysis.

Small, Christopher. *The Road to Miniluv: George Orwell, the State, and God.* Pittsburgh: University of Pittsburgh Press, 1976.

Small's text takes a biocritical look at the sources and ideas that informed the creation of *Nineteen Eighty-Four*.

Stansky, Peter, ed. *On* Nineteen Eighty-Four. New York: W.H. Freeman, 1983.

Edited by the first of Orwell's biographers, this is one of a handful of enduring essay collections published around the year 1984 to consider Orwell's dystopian text. Stansky's contains a comprehensive reading bibliography.

Stansky, Peter, and William Abrahams. *The Unknown Orwell.* London: Constable & Co., 1972.

———. *Orwell: The Transformation.* London: Constable & Co., 1979.

Taken together, these two volumes chronicle Orwell's life up to the period of the Spanish Civil War. However, as Shelden (*q.v.*) points out, "Sonia Orwell was adamantly opposed and refused to allow them to quote from her husband's works." Thus, although their work represents the first large-scale biographical effort to canvas numerous sources and review holdings at the major repositories of Orwell papers, the voice of the subject is conspicuously absent.

Steinhoff, William. *George Orwell and the Origins of* 1984. Ann Arbor: University of Michigan Press, 1975.

Concerned with the intellectual, artistic, and political influences which shaped Orwell and led to his writing *Nineteen Eighty-Four*, Steinhoff's work is cited in the majority of Orwell scholarship of the past three decades.

Contributors

Harold Bloom is Sterling Professor of the Humanities at Yale University and Henry W. and Albert A. Berg Professor of English at the New York University Graduate School. He is the author of over 20 books, including *Shelley's Mythmaking* (1959), *The Visionary Company* (1961), *Blake's Apocalypse* (1963), *Yeats* (1970), *A Map of Misreading* (1975), *Kabbalah and Criticism* (1975), *Agon: Toward a Theory of Revisionism* (1982), *The American Religion* (1992), *The Western Canon* (1994), and *Omens of Millennium: The Gnosis of Angels, Dreams, and Resurrection* (1996). *The Anxiety of Influence* (1973) sets forth Professor Bloom's provocative theory of the literary relationships between the great writers and their predecessors. His most recent books include *Shakespeare: The Invention of the Human* (1998), a 1998 National Book Award finalist, *How to Read and Why* (2000), *Genius: A Mosaic of One Hundred Exemplary Creative Minds* (2002), and *Hamlet: Poem Unlimited* (2003). In 1999, Professor Bloom received the prestigious American Academy of Arts and Letters Gold Medal for Criticism, and in 2002 he received the Catalonia International Prize.

Gabriel Welsch's short stories, poems, and reviews have appeared in *Georgia Review*, *Mid-American Review*, *Crab Orchard Review*, and *Cream City Review*. He regularly reviews literature for *Harvard Review*, *Missouri Review*, *Slope*, and *Small Press Review*. He received a Pennsylvania Council on the Arts Fellowship for Literature in fiction in 2003.

Stephen Spender was born in 1909 in London, attended Oxford University, and fought in the Spanish Civil War. In the 1920s and 1930s he associated with other poets and socialists, such as W.H. Auden, Christopher Isherwood, Louis MacNeice, and C. Day Lewis, and his early poetry was often inspired by social protest. During World War II, Spender worked for the London fire service. He co-founded the magazine *Horizon* with

Cyril Connolly and served as its editor from 1939 until 1941. He was editor of *Encounter* from 1953 until 1966. Spender's books of poetry include *Twenty Poems, Vienna, The Still Centre, Poems of Dedication*, and *The Generous Days*. Spender was a professor of English at University College, London, from 1970 until 1977, and he gave frequent lecture tours in the United States. He was knighted in 1983, and he died in 1995.

Gorman Beauchamp is an adjunct associate professor of English at the University of Michigan. His writings include *Jack London* and articles on Shakespeare, Swift, Wordsworth, Melville, Twain, Wells, Zamyatin, Huxley, Orwell, Faulkner, and others.

Paul R. Ehrlich and Anne H. Ehrlich are best known for their environmental advocacy, particularly in the area of population. Paul Ehrlich is the author of nearly forty books, including the influential 1968 study *The Population Bomb* and its follow-up, 1990's *The Population Explosion*, co-written with Anne Ehrlich. Their recent books written together include *Healing the Planet, The Stork and the Plow, Betrayal of Science and Reason*, and *Human Natures: Genes, Cultures and the Human Prospect*. Paul Ehrlich is Bing Professor of Population Studies in the Department of Biological Sciences at Stanford University, and Anne Ehrlich is a senior research associate at Stanford University and associate director of Stanford's Center for Conservation Biology.

Ian Watt, a former professor of English at Stanford University, was the author of numerous articles and several books on literary theory, most notably *The Rise of the Novel* and *Conrad in the Nineteenth Century*.

Joseph Adelson is an emeritus professor of psychology at the University of Michigan and a clinical psychologist. His work in the field, which has centered on adolescence and adult psychopathology, has been immensely influential.

Richard W. Bailey is Fred Newton Scott Collegiate Professor of English Language and Literature at the University of Michigan. He is the author of editor of several books, including *Milestones in the History of English in America: Papers by Allen Walker Read*; *Nineteenth-Century English*; *The Oxford Companion to the English Language*; *Images of English: A Cultural History of the Language*; *Early Modern English: Additions and Antedatings to the Record of English Vocabulary, 1475-1700*; and *Computer Poems*.

Alex Zwerdling is Professor of English at the University of California, Berkeley, specializing in modern British and American literature. He is the author of *Virginia Woolf and the Real World*, *Improvised Europeans: American Literary Expatriates in London*, and *Orwell and the Left*.

Bernard Crick is Emeritus Professor of Birkbeck College, University of London. His books include, *George Orwell: A Life*; *The American Science of Politics*; *In Defence of Politics*; *Essays on Politics and Literature*; *Political Thoughts and Polemics*; and, most recently, *Democracy: A Very Short Introduction*. Joint editor of the *Political Quarterly* from 1965 until 1980, now literary editor, he has written for the *Observer*, the *Guardian*, the *New Statesman*, the *Scotsman*, and the *Independent*.

Hugh Kenner is best known for his classic studies of literary modernism, including *The Pound Era* and *The Mechanic Muse*. He has also authored books on technology and media, including *Bucky: A Guided Tour of Buckminster Fuller* and *Chuck Jones: A Flurry of Drawings*. His most recent book, *The Elsewhere Community*, is a quasi-autobiographical account of the role of travel in the making of art.

Joan Weatherly is a former president of the Southeastern Conference on Linguistics. She has spoken on Orwellian topics at numerous conferences, including those of the Society for Utopian Studies, the Society for Cross-Cultural Research, the Association for the Study of Literature and Environment, and the Nineteenth Century Studies Association. She was teaching in the Department of English at the University of Memphis when she wrote "The Death of Big Sister: Orwell's Tragic Message."

Michael P. Zuckert is Nancy Reeves Dreux Professor of Government and International Studies at the University of Notre Dame. He is the author of *Natural Rights and the New Republicanism*, *The Natural Rights Republic* (named an Outstanding Book for 1997 by *Choice Magazine*) and *Launching Liberalism: On Lochean Political Philosophy*, as well as many articles on a variety of topics, including George Orwell, Plato's *Apology*, Shakespeare, and contemporary liberal theory.

Michael Shelden is the author of biographies of George Orwell, Graham Greene, and Cyril Connelly and is a professor of English at Indiana State University. He writes regularly on a variety of aspects of literary and popular culture for such newspapers as *The London Telegraph*, *The Washington Post*, and *The Baltimore Sun*.

Stephen Ingle has been Head of the Politics Department at the University of Stirling in Scotland since moving from the University of Hull in 1991. His academic interests center on the relationship between politics and literature and on adversarial (two-party) political systems, especially in the United Kingdom and Australasia. He has written two books in his first area of interest, *Socialist Thought in Imaginative Literature* and *George Orwell: A Political Life*, and two in the second: *Parliament and Health Politics* and *The British Party System*.

Acknowledgments

The Creative Element: A Study of Vision, Despair and Orthodoxy among Some Modern Writers by Stephen Spender. London: Hamish Hamilton, 1953: pp. 137–138. © 1953 by Hamish Hamilton, Ltd. Reprinted by permission.

George Orwell, letter to Francis A. Henson (16 June 1949). From *Collected Essays, Journalism and Letters of George Orwell*. Eds. Sonia Orwell and Ian Angus. New York: Harcourt Brace Jovanovich, 1968: Vol. 4, p. 502. © 1968 by Sonia Brownell Orwell. Reprinted by permission.

"Of Man's Last Disobedience: Zamyatin's *We* and Orwell's *1984*," by Gordon Beauchamp. From *Comparative Literature Studies* 10, no. 4 (December 1973): pp. 293–294. © 1973 by The Board of Trustees of the University of Illinois. Reprinted by permission.

"1984: Population and Environment," by Paul R. Ehrlich and Anne H. Ehrlich. From *On* Nineteen Eighty-Four. Ed. Peter Stansky. New York: W.H. Freeman & Co., 1983: pp. 49–51. © 1983 by Stanford Alumni Association. Reprinted by permission.

"Winston Smith: The Last Humanist," by Ian Watt. From *On* Nineteen Eighty-Four. Ed. Peter Stansky. New York: W.H. Freeman & Co., 1983: pp. 104–108. © 1983 by Stanford Alumni Association. Reprinted by permission.

"The Self and Memory in *Nineteen Eighty-Four*," by Joseph Adelson. From *The Future of* Nineteen Eighty-Four. Ed. Ejner J. Jensen. Ann Arbor: University of Michigan Press, 1984: pp. 112–118. © 1984 by the University of Michigan. Reprinted by permission.

"George Orwell and the English Language," by Richard W. Bailey. From *The Future of* Nineteen Eighty-Four. Ed. Ejner J. Jensen. Ann Arbor: University of Michigan Press, 1984, pp. 24–28. © 1984 by the University of Michigan. Reprinted by permission.

"Orwell's Psychopolitics," by Alex Zwerdling. From *The Future of* Nineteen Eighty-Four. Ed. Ejner J. Jensen. Ann Arbor: University of Michigan Press, 1984: pp. 90–95, 98–101. © 1984 by the University of Michigan. Reprinted by permission.

"Reading *Nineteen Eighty-Four* as Satire," by Bernard Crick. From *Reflections of America, 1984: An Orwell Symposium.* Athens: University of Georgia Press, 1986: pp. 22–26. © 1986 by the University of Georgia Press. Reprinted by permission.

"The Politics of the Plain Style," by Hugh Kenner. From *Reflections of America, 1984: An Orwell Symposium.* Athens: University of Georgia Press, 1986: pp. 63–65. © 1986 by the University of Georgia Press. Reprinted by permission.

"The Death of Big Sister: Orwell's Tragic Message," by Joan Weatherly. From *Critical Essays on George Orwell.* Eds. Bernard Oldsey and Joseph Browne. Boston: G.K. Hall & Co., 1986: pp. 80–83. © 1986 by Bernard Oldsey and Joseph Browne. Reprinted by permission.

"Orwell's Hopes and Fears," by Michael P. Zuckert. From *The Orwellian Moment: Hindsight and Foresight in the Post-1984 World.* Eds. Robert L. Savage, James Combs, Dan Nimmo. Fayetteville: University of Arkansas Press, 1989: pp. 55–57. © 1989 by Robert L. Savage, James Combs, and Dan Nimmo. Reprinted by permission.

Orwell: The Authorized Biography by Michael Shelden. London: William Heinemann Ltd., 1991: pp. 470–472. © 1991 by Michael Shelden. Reprinted by permission.

George Orwell: A Political Life by Stephen Ingle. Manchester: Manchester University Press, 1993: pp. 95–99. © 1993 by Stephen Ingle. Reprinted by permission.

Index

118